LOVE POEMS

LOVE POEMS

from
Spain & Spanish America

Selected and Translated by
PERRY HIGMAN

City Lights Books
San Francisco

©Translations 1986 by Perry Higman

Cover painting "Lovers" by Felix Jiménez Chino (1979) by courtesy of
The Selden Rodman Collection of Popular Art, Oakland, New Jersey.

Library of Congress Cataloging-in-Publication Data

Main entry under title

Love poems.

Bibliography: p.
        1. Love poetry, Spanish—Translations into English. 2. Love
poetry, Spanish American—Translations into English. 3. Love poetry,
English—Translations from Spanish. 4. Love poetry, Spanish. 5. Love
poetry, Spanish American. I. Higman, Perry
PQ6267.E5L64 1986   861'.04'08354   85-29158
ISBN 0-87286-185-6
ISSSSSSBN 0-87286-183-X (pbk)

City Lights Books are available to bookstores through our primary
distributor: Subterranean Company. P.O. Box 160, 265 S. 5th St.,
Monroe, OR 97456. 541-847-5274. Toll-free orders 800-274-7826.
FAX 541-847-6018. Our books are also available through library
jobbers and regional distributors. For personal orders and catalogs,
please write to City Lights Books, 261 Columbus Avenue,
San Francisco, CA 94133.

CITY LIGHTS BOOKS are edited by Lawrence Ferlinghetti and
Nancy J. Peters and published at the City Lights Bookstore,
261 Columbus Avenue, San Francisco, CA 94133.

Love is the only explanation of our survival. Through the ages it has inspired poets to combat the implacable siege of hatred, destruction and death with their song. Our most primitive sources of learning—mythology is one of them—teach us that Chaos received cosmic ordination from the actions of the first gods: the Earth (Gaea) and Love (Eros). Love is, then, the great element of creation that preserves our existence and our enduring hopes for an ever better world for all humanity.

Julio Durán-Cerda

TRANSLATOR'S INTRODUCTION

The Spanish poet Pedro Salinas talks of "the poem born in man's solitude" that later becomes a "unifying force" among all human beings. I conceived this collection of love poems in that spirit. These are poems I keep coming back to time after time because with each renewed contact they strike chords of understanding and kinship with their varied expressions of love, and with each reading I find new meaning. They are some of the best poems by the best Hispanic poets. The teachers who helped me understand them, my friends who have talked with me about them, and the students I've taught and learned from have shown me that love poems truly are a unifying force among us all. They speak to us through their beauty, strength and feeling; they reveal our sympathies; they show us our common humanity; they are timeless.

My goal in these translations was to re-create the original poem, to give it that identity which most becomes it in English. I hope I have provided the English reader an opportunity to share these poems' beauty and meaning that transcends temporal, cultural, or linguistic differences.

I must name some of my colleagues and friends who shared their effort and skill with me in this work. Lynn C. Jacox, who did several of the translations, served on the Montana Arts Council as poetry consultant in the Montana Public Schools before her current position as Program Director for the Women's Program at Eastern Washington University. She is a poet who provided immeasurable help with the planning and accomplishment of the project. My gratitude to Joseph Ricapito who taught me that literature could be enjoyed and loved; to Julio Durán-Cerda at the University of Iowa whose knowledge and perception echo through the whole book; to Sandra Higman for years of sharing poetry and these poems; to Delrene Bareither for help on early versions of the translations; to Bea and Chet Higman for research and proofreading; to Jeanne Sparks for much, much typing; and to Eastern Washington University for time to work on the project. Many thanks also to Nancy Peters at City Lights Books for her fine editing of the manuscripts.

Perry Higman

ACKNOWLEDGMENTS

The translator wishes to thank the following for permission to reprint selections that appear in this book:

Rafael Alberti. "Para Aitana," "Retornos del amor en los vívidos paisajes," from *Poesías completas*, ©Editorial Losada, S.A., Buenos Aires, 1961. Reprinted by permission of Agencia Literaria Carmen Balcells.

Vicente Aleixandre. "Padre mío," "Mano entregada," "Como la mar, los besos," "Que nacioí muerta," "Más allá," from *Poesías completas*, ©Vicente Aleixandre, 1966, Aguilar, S.A. de Ediciones, 1968. Reprinted by permission of Agencia Literaria Carmen Balcells.

Emilio Ballagas. "Elegía de María Belén Chacón," from *Orbita de Emilio Ballagas*, ©Unión de Escritores y Artistas de Cuba, 1965.

Jorge Luis Borges. "Amorosa anticipación," from *Obra poética*, ©Emecé Editores, S.A., Buenos Aires, 1967.

Luis Cernuda. "Unos cuerpos son como flores," from *La realidad y el deseo, 1924-1962*, ©1958 Fondo de cultura económica.

Baldomero Fernández Moreno. "Habla la madre castellana," from *Poesía*, ©1928, L.J. Rosso, Buenos Aires.

Jorge Guillén. "Los fieles amantes," "Cima de la delicia," from *Selección de poemas*, ©Jorge Guillén, 1965, Editorial Gredos, S.A., Madrid, España.

Nicolás Guillén. "Búcate plata," "Bares," from *Antología mayor*, ©1964, Ediciones Unión, La Habana. Reprinted by permission of Unión de Escritores y Artistas de Cuba.

Miguel Hernández. "Cantar," "El amor ascendía entre nosotros," from *Obra poética completa*, ©Herederos de Miguel Hernández, ©Zero, 1976. Reprinted by permission of Josefina Manresa Marhuenda.

Juana de Ibarbourou. "Madrugada," "La caricia," "Tiempo," from *Obras completas*, Copyright 1953, by Aguilar, S.A. de Ediciones, Madrid.

Juan Ramón Jiménez. "Cuando, dormida tú, me echo en tu alma," "Vino, primero, pura," "Mirlo fiel," from *Páginas escogidas*, ©Editorial Gredos, Madrid, 1958.

Ramón López Verlade. "Mi prima Agueda," from *Poesías completas*, ©1968 by Ramón López Velarde. Reprinted by permission of Editorial Porrúa.

CONTENTS

Delmira Agustini

born in Montevideo, Uruguay, 1887
died in Montevideo, July, 1914

One of Uruguay's great poets, Delmira Agustini combines in her poems traditional Spanish forms and meters with spiritual and erotic feeling. Her imagery, spontaneous to the point of being "careless and of questionable taste" according to some critics, has endured precisely because of its shocking sincerity. Thanks in part to Rubén Darío's fervent praise of her work, she gained early recognition for her literary talent. In 1914, the year she was working on what would prove to be her most popular collections, *Los cálices vacíos* and *El rosario de Eros*, she married, but within a few weeks she left her husband. She consented to see him one last time. The next day, word spread through Montevideo that Agustini had been found dead in one of the city's *casas para citas* (assignation hotels) alongside the body of her husband, who had apparently shot her and then himself.

Delmira Agustini
EXPLOSION

¡Si la vida es amor, bendita sea!
¡Quiero más vida para amar! Hoy siento
que no valen mil años de la idea
lo que un minuto azul del sentimiento.

Mi corazón moría triste y lento...
Hoy abre en luz como una flor febea.
¡La vida brota como un mar violento
donde la mano del amor golpea!

Hoy partió hacia la noche, triste, fría,
rotas las alas mi melancolía;
como una vieja mancha de dolor

en la sombra lejana se deslíe...
¡Mi vida toda canta, besa, ríe!
¡Mi vida toda es una boca en flor!

4

Delmira Agustini
EXPLOSION

If life is love, blessed be it!
I want more life to love! Today I feel
a thousand years of ideas are worth nothing
next to one azure minute of feeling.

My heart was dying, sad and slow . . .
Now it blooms in light like a flower of Phoebus:
Life bursts like a violent sea
where the hand of love strikes its blow!

Today my melancholy, with broken wings
went out into the night, sad, cold;
like an old mark of sorrow

it dissolves in distant shadows . . .
My whole life laughs, kisses, sings!
My whole life is a mouth in bloom!

from *El libro blanco,* 1907
P.H.

Delmira Agustini
OTRA ESTIRPE

Eros, yo quiero guiarte, Padre ciego . . .
pido a tus manos todopoderosas
¡su cuerpo excelso derramado en fuego
sobre mi cuerpo desmayado en rosas!

La eléctrica corola que hoy despliego
brinda el nectario de un jardín de Esposas;
para sus buitres en mi carne entrego
todo un enjambre de palomas rosas.

Da a las dos sierpes de su abrazo, crueles,
mi gran tallo febril . . . Absintio, mieles,
viérteme de sus venas, de su boca . . .

¡Así tendida, soy un surco ardiente
donde puede nutrirse la simiente
de otra Estirpe sublimemente loca!

Delmira Agustini
ANOTHER LINEAGE

Eros, blind Father, let me show you the way . . .
I beg of your all-powerful hands
his sublime body poured in flame
over my body fainted in roses!

The electric corolla I unfold today
offers the nectary of a garden of wives;
in my flesh I surrender to his birds of prey
a whole swarm of rose-colored doves.

Give the two cruel serpents of his embrace,
my tall feverish stalk . . . Honey, absinthe,
pour on me from his mouth, from his veins . . .

Lying here before him, I am a burning furrow
that can nourish the seed
of another Breed sublimely insane!

from *Los cálices vacíos*, 1913
P.H.

Rafael Alberti

born in Puerto de Santa María (Cádiz),
Spain, December 2, 1902

Rafael Alberti intended to become a painter, and in fact he has
painted as well as written poetry all his life. His poems show the
influence of Góngora's elaborate sensual imagery as well as that of
the French surrealists. The result is a combination of vivid physical
images expressed with dreamlike, strongly personal lyricism.
He began writing at 19, and his first book, *Marinero en tierra* won
Spain's National Prize for Literature in 1925. In 1929, he participated
in demonstrations against Primo de Rivera's dictatorship, beginning
a life-long commitment to progressive politics. In 1930 he married
María Teresa León. During the Spanish civil war he enlisted as an
aviator with the Republican army; after the war he settled in Buenos
Aires, where his daughter Aitana was born in 1941. He returned to
Spain after Franco's death and lives now in Madrid.

Rafael Alberti
PARA AITANA

(9 de agosto de 1956)

Aitana, niña mía, baja la primavera
para ti quince flores pequeñas y graciosas.
Sigues siendo de aire, siguen todas tus cosas
siendo como encantadas por una luz ligera.

Aitana, niña mía, fuera yo quien moviera
para ti eternamente las auras más dichosas,
quien peinara más luces y alisara más rosas
en tus pequeñas alas de brisa mensajera.

Aitana, niña mía, ya que eres aire y eres
como el aire y remontas el aire como quieres,
feliz, callada y ciega y sola en tu alegría,

aunque para tus alas yo te abriera más cielo,
no olvides que hasta puede deshojarse en un vuelo
el aire, niña Aitana, Aitana, niña mía.

Rafael Alberti
FOR AITANA
(9th of August, 1956)

Aitana, my child, Springtime bows
to give you fifteen small and delicate flowers.
You are still fashioned from air, and all your things
still seem charmed by a fragile light.

Aitana, my child, how I wish I could make
the fairest winds blow forever for you,
and that I could comb more lights and smooth out
                                    more roses
on your young wings of messenger breeze.

Aitana, my child, since you are air and are
like air and you soar off on the wind when you wish,
happy, hushed and blind and alone in your bliss,

though I'd open new skies to your wings,
don't forget that even the air can lose its leaves in a flash,
the air, dear child Aitana, Aitana, my child.

from *Poemas diversos*; *1945-1959* in *Poesías completas*, 1961
P.H.

Rafael Alberti
RETORNOS DEL AMOR EN
LOS VIVIDOS PAISAJES

Creemos, amor mío, que aquellos paisajes
se quedaron dormidos o muertos con nosotros
en la edad, en el día en que los habitamos;
que los árboles pierden la memoria
y las noches se van, dando al olvido
lo que las hizo hermosas y tal vez inmortales.

Pero basta el más leve palpitar de una hoja,
una estrella borrada que respira de pronto
para vernos los mismos alegres que llenamos
los lugares que juntos nos tuvieron.
Y así despiertas hoy, mi amor, a mi costado,
entre los groselleros y las fresas ocultas
al amparo del firme corazón de los bosques.

Allí está la caricia mojada de rocío,
las briznas delicadas que refrescan tu lecho,
los silfos encantados de ornar tu cabellera
y las altas ardillas misteriosas que llueven
sobre tu sueño el verde menudo de las ramas.

Sé feliz, hoja, siempre: nunca tengas otoño,
hoja que me has traído
con tu temblor pequeño
el aroma de tanta ciega edad luminosa.
Y tú, mínima estrella perdida que me abres
las íntimas ventanas de mis noches mãs jóvenes,
nunca cierres tu lumbre
sobre tantas alcobas que al alba nos durmieron
y aquella biblioteca con la luna
y los libros aquellos dulcemente caídos
y los montes afuera desvelados cantándonos.

Rafael Alberti
RETURNINGS OF LOVE
IN VIVID LANDSCAPES

We believe, my love, that those landscapes
were left sleeping or lifeless with us
in the years, in the days when we lived in them;
that trees lose their memory
and the nights fade away, slipping into oblivion
with what made them beautiful and perhaps immortal.

But the slightest fluttering of a leaf is enough,
a vanished star that suddenly takes a breath,
to see ourselves the same happy lovers who filled
the places that embraced us both.
And so you awaken today, my love, at my side,
among the currants and hidden strawberries
in the shelter of the firm heart of the woods.

There is the damp caress of dew,
the delicate wood chips that freshen your bed,
the sylphs enchanted with adorning your hair
and the high mysterious squirrels that rain
upon your sleep the green bits of the branches.

Be happy, leaf, always; may you never see autumn,
leaf that has brought me
with your tiny trembling
the aroma of so many blind luminous years.
And you, smallest lost star that opens
the intimate windows of my most youthful nights,
may you never put out your light
over all of the bedrooms that saw us to sleep at dawn
and that library in the moonlight
and those books sweetly fallen there
and the wakeful mountains singing to us afar.

from *Retornos de lo vivo lejano*, 1952
P.H.

13

Vicente Aleixandre   *born in Seville, Spain, April 26, 1898*

died in Madrid, December 13, 1984

Vicente Aleixandre's poems, centered in love and death, express both the anguish and hope of mankind. His uniquely individual style is strongly influenced by French surrealism, by Góngora, and by an exploration of language reminiscent of Quevedo. The son of a railroad engineer, he had an older sister and brother who died early in childhood, and another sister Sofía who was stillborn. He lived with a surviving sister most of his life. While studying law in Madrid he fell seriously ill, and during his convalescence he started writing poetry. Openly sympathetic to the Republic, he remained in Spain through the civil war but did not fight because of ill health. In 1935 his *La destrucción o el amor* won the National Prize for Literature, and he was awarded the Nobel Prize for Literature in 1977.

Vicente Aleixandre
PADRE MIO

(A mi hermana)

Lejos estás, padre mío, allá en tu reino de las sombras.
Mira a tu hijo, oscuro en esta tiniebla huérfana,
lejos de la benévola luz de tus ojos continuos.
Allí nací, crecí: de aquella luz pura
tomé vida, y aquel fulgor sereno
se embebió en esta forma, que todavía despide,
como un eco apagado, tu luz resplandeciente.

Bajo la frente poderosa, mundo entero de vida,
mente completa que un humano alcanzara,
sentí la sombra que protegió mi infancia. Leve, leve,
resbaló así la niñez como alígero pie sobre
                              una yerba noble
y si besé a los pájaros, si pude posar mis labios
sobre tantas alas fugaces que una aurora empujara,
fue por ti, por tus benévolos ojos que presidieron
                              mi nacimiento
y fueron como brazos que por encima de mi testa cernían
la luz, la luz tranquila, no heridora a mis ojos de niño.

Alto, padre, como una montaña que pudiera inclinarse,
que pudiera vencerse sobre mi propia frente descuidada
y besarme tan luminosamente, tan silenciosa y puramente
como la luz que pasa por las crestas radiantes
donde reina el azul de los cielos purísimos.

Por tu pecho bajaba una cascada luminosa de bondad,
                              que tocaba
luego mi rostro y bañaba mi cuerpo aún infantil,
                              que emergía
de tu fuerza tranquila como desnudo, reciente,
nacido cada día de ti, porque tú fuiste padre
diario, y cada día yo nací de tu pecho, exhalado
de tu amor, como acaso mensaje de tu seno purísimo.

16

Vicente Aleixandre
MY FATHER

(To my sister)

You are far away, my father, there in your realm of shadows.
Look at your son, dark in this orphan twilight,
far from the benevolent light of your continuous eyes.
I was born there; grew up there; from that pure light
I took life, and that serene radiance
was absorbed into this form, which still says goodbye,
like a muffled echo, to your splendorous light.

Beneath your powerful brow, whole world of life,
a complete mind achieved by a man,
I felt the shadow that protected my infancy. Swift, swift,
my childhood slipped by this way like a winged foot
on noble grass,
and if I kissed the birds, if I could rest my lips
upon as many fleeting wings as a dawn could set
in motion,
it was because of you, for your benevolent eyes that presided
over my birth
and were like arms above my head that sifted
the light, the tranquil light, harmless to my child eyes.

Tall, father, like a mountain that could bend low,
in complete control above my own careless brow
and kiss me as luminously, as silently and purely
as the light that spreads through radiant crests
where blue rules immaculate skies.

From your breast poured a bright cascade of kindness,
that then touched
my face and bathed my body still new, come
from your tranquil strength as if naked, recent,
born each day from you, because you were a father
daily, and each day I was born from your breast, exhaled
from your love, as perhaps a message from your pure heart.

17

Porque yo nací entero cada día, entero y tierno siempre,
y débil y gozoso cada día hollé naciendo
la yerba misma intacta: pisé leve, estrené brisas,
henchí también mi seno, y miré el mundo
y lo vi bueno. Bueno tú, padre mío, mundo mío, tú solo.

Hasta la orilla del mar condujiste mi mano.
Benévolo y potente tú como un bosque en la orilla,
yo sentí mis espaldas guardadas contra el viento estrellado.
Pude sumergir mi cuerpo reciente cada aurora
                                    en la espuma,
y besar a la mar candorosa en el día,
siempre olvidada, siempre, de su noche de lutos.

Padre, tú me besaste con los labios de azul sereno.
Limpios de nubes veía yo tus ojos,
aunque a veces un velo de tristeza eclipsaba a mi frente
esa luz que sin duda de los cielos tomabas.
Oh padre altísimo, oh tierno padre gigantesco
que así, en los brazos, desvalido, me hubiste.
Huérfano de ti, menudo como entonces, caído sobre
                                    una yerba triste,
heme hoy aquí, padre, sobre el mundo en tu ausencia,
mientras pienso en tu forma sagrada, habitadora acaso
                                    de una sombra amorosa,
por la que nunca, nunca tu corazón me olvida.

Oh padre mío, seguro estoy que en la tiniebla fuerte
tú vives y me amas. Que un vigor poderoso,
un latir, aún revienta en la tierra.
Y que unas ondas de pronto, desde un fondo, sacuden
a la tierra y la ondulan, y a mis pies se estremece.

Pero yo soy de carne todavía. Y mi vida
es de carne, padre, padre mío. Y aquí estoy,
solo, sobre la tierra quieta, menudo como entonces,
                                    sin verte,
derribado sobre los inmensos brazos que horriblemente
                                    te imitan.

Since I was born whole each day, always whole and tender,
fragile and joyful each day anew I would tread
the grass itself untouched: I stepped lightly, premiered
                              the breezes,
swelled my breast as well, and I looked at the world
and saw it good. Good you, my father, my world, you alone.

To the shores of the sea you guided my hand.
Kind and strong you like a forest on shore,
I felt you shield my back from the starry wind.
I could submerge my new body each dawn in the spray,
and kiss the candorous sea by day,
always forgetful, always, of its mournful night.

Father, you kissed me with lips of serene blue.
Free of clouds I saw your eyes,
Yet sometimes a veil of sadness eclipsed from my brow
that light you were doubtless taking from the skies.
Oh father most high, oh tender giant father,
this is the way, in your arms, helpless, you held me.
Orphaned from you, small as then, fallen on some
                              sad blade of grass,
here you have me, father, on the world in your absence,
while I ponder your sacred form, chance inhabitant
                              of some loving shadow,
through which your heart never, never forgets me.

Oh my father, I am certain that in the strong twilight
you live and love me. That a powerful vigor,
a throbbing, still bursts within the earth.
And that sudden waves, from some deep place, shake
the earth and make it quake, and my feet tremble.

But I am still made of flesh. And my life
is of flesh, father, my father. And here I am,
alone, upon the quiet earth, small as ever, without seeing you,
cast down upon immense arms that horribly mimic you.

from *Sombra del paraíso*; *1939-1943*, 1943
P.H.

Vicente Aleixandre
MANO ENTREGADA

Pero otro día toco tu mano. Mano tibia.
Tu delicada mano silente. A veces cierro
mis ojos y toco leve tu mano, leve toque
que comprueba su forma, que tienta
su estructura, sintiendo bajo la piel alada el duro hueso
insobornable, el triste hueso adonde no llega nunca
el amor, Oh carne dulce, que sí se empapa
                              del amor hermoso.

Es por la piel secreta, secretamente abierta,
                              invisiblemente entreabierta,
por donde el calor tibio propaga su voz, su afán dulce;
por donde mi voz penetra hasta tus venas tibias,
para rodar por ellas en tu escondida sangre,
como otra sangre que sonara oscura, que dulcemente
                              oscura te besara
por dentro, recorriendo despacio como sonido puro
ese cuerpo, que ahora resuena mío, mío, poblado
                              de mis voces profundas,
oh resonado cuerpo de mi amor, oh poseído cuerpo,
    oh cuerpo sólo sonido de mi voz poseyéndole.

Por eso, cuando acaricio tu mano, sé que sólo
                              el hueso rehúsa
mi amor—el nunca incandescente hueso del hombre—.
Y que una zona triste de tu ser se rehúsa,
mientras tu carne entera llega un instante lúcido
en que total flamea, por virtud de ese lento contacto
                              de tu mano,
de tu porosa mano suavísima que gime,
tu delicada mano silente, por donde entro
despacio, despacísimo, secretamente en tu vida,
hasta tus venas hondas donde bogo,
donde te pueblo y canto completo entre tu carne.

Vicente Aleixandre
YOUR HAND IN MINE

But another day I touch your hand. Warm hand.
Your delicate silent hand. Sometimes I close
my eyes and lightly touch your hand, a light touch
that confirms its form, that traces
its structure, feeling beneath the winged skin
the hard uncorruptible bone, the sad bone where love
never reaches. Oh sweet flesh, so drenched
                        in beautiful love.

It's through your secret skin, secretly open, invisibly ajar,
where the warm heat spreads its voice, its sweet desire;
where my voice penetrates clear into your warm veins,
to roam through them in your hidden blood,
like another blood that echoes dark, sweetly dark
                        kisses you
from within, traveling slowly like pure sound
through that body, which now resounds mine, mine,
                        peopled with my deepest words,
oh resonant body of my love, oh possessed body, oh body
                        only a sound of
my voice possessing you.

And so, when I caress your hand, I know only
                        the bone refuses
my love—the never incandescent bone of man—.
And that a sad zone of your being refuses,
while your whole flesh reaches a lucid instant
bursts all into flame, by that slow contact
                        with your hand,
of your porous hand so soft which moans,
your delicate silent hand, where I enter
slowly, very slowly, secretly into your life,
clear into your deepest veins where I forge my way,
where I people you and sing you full within your flesh.

from *Historia del corazón*; *1945-1953*, 1954
P.H.

Vicente Aleixandre
COMO LA MAR, LOS BESOS

No importan los emblemas
ni las vanas palabras que son un soplo sólo.
Importa el eco de lo que oí y escucho.
Tu voz, que muerta vive, como yo que al pasar
aquí aún te hallo.

Eras más consistente,
más duradera, no porque te besase,
ni porque, firme, en ti tuve así a la existencia.
Sino porque como la mar
después que arena invade temerosa se ahonda.
En verdes o en espumas la mar, feliz, se aleja.
Como ella fue y volvió tú nunca vuelves.

Quizá porque, rodada
sobre playa sin fin, no pude hallarte.
La huella de tu espuma,
cuando el agua se va, queda en los bordes.

Sólo bordes encuentro. Sólo el filo de voz que
en mí quedara.
Como un alga tus besos.
Mágicos en la luz, pues muertos tornan.

Vicente Aleixandre
LIKE THE SEA, KISSES

Emblems mean nothing
nor vain words that are but breaths of air.
What matters is the echo of what I heard and listen to.
Your voice, though dead lives, as I who pass
here still find you.

You were more consistent,
more lasting, not because I kissed you,
nor because with you, firm, I held fast to existence.
Rather because like the sea
after invading the sand deepens, fearful.
In greens or in foam the sea, joyful, grows distant.
As it ebbed and flowed, you never return.

Perhaps because, rolled
on an endless shore, I could not find you.
The traces of your foam,
when the water recedes, remain along the edges.

I only find edges. Only the fine edge of a voice that
remains in me.
Like a bit of seaweed your kisses.
Magical in the light, then they turn lifeless.

from *Poemas varios*; *1927-1967*, 1968
P.H.

Vicente Aleixandre
... QUE NACIÓ MUERTA

(Mi hermana Sofía)

Lejana está. Muy lejos.
Como en ese cestillo
que en el Nilo perdióse:
Moisés (moisés le llaman),
entre juncos un día,
las aguas, un lucero
y los remeros negros
desnudos en la noche,
bogando. El son es triste.

Pero tú no naciste
así, Sofía, niña
que una mano tomara
largamente de un fondo
para lanzarla rauda
en la corriente fría
que nunca desemboca.
Ah, sí, tú no naciste
sino cestillo en agua,
sin remos ni lucero,
sin llegada, ni arriba
la enorme luna ardiendo.
Una mano segura
te lanzó y navegaste,
cuerpo yerto naciendo
en esta orilla muda
donde muerta arribaste.
Yo lo supe de niño.
Como niña que llega
y en ciego borde atraca,
yo supe que el cestillo
fue recogido y muerta
viviste, pues nacías.
Sofía fue tu nombre,
sobre tu frente helada,
en ese crisma inmenso
de un arribo entre juncos.

Vicente Aleixandre
... WHO WAS BORN DEAD

(My sister Sophia)

She is far away. Very far.
Like in that small basket
that was lost in the Nile:
Moses (moses they call him),
among the bulrushes one day,
the waters, a bright star
and the black boatmen
naked in the night,
rowing. A sad sound.

But you were not born
that way, Sophia, child
that a hand drew
slowly from some deep place
to cast her impetuous
into the cold current
that never reaches the sea.
Ah, yes, you were not born
save as a basket in the water,
without oars or star,
without arrival, or above
the enormous moon burning.
A firm hand
cast off and you sailed,
stiff body being born
on this silent shore
where you arrived dead.
I found out as a child.
Like a little girl that arrives
and docks at the blind water's edge,
I learned that the little basket
was recovered and dead
you lived, for you were born.
Sophia was your name,
upon your icy forehead,
in that immense chrisom
of an arrival among the bulrushes.

Sofía, sí, sabiendo,
en tus ojos cerrados,
la ciencia de un viaje
súbito: vida entera
que fue nacer a muerte.
Sabia Sofía inmóvil
en la orilla durmiendo,
sin que nunca latieras
a la luz: tu luz, dentro.
Sofía, hermana, niña
que un niño oyó: Mi hermana
que no habló, y aún te escucho.

Sophia, yes, knowing,
within your closed eyes,
the knowledge of a sudden
journey: an entire life
that was, to be born to death.
Wise Sophia, still,
on the bank sleeping,
without ever throbbing
in the light: your light, within.
Sophia, sister, child
a small boy heard: My sister
who did not speak, but I listen to you yet.

from *Retratos con nombre*; *1958-1964,* 1965
P.H.

Vicente Aleixandre
MÁS ALLÁ

Más allá de la vida, mi amor, más allá siempre,
ahora ligeros, únicos, sobre un lecho de estrellas,
poblamos a la noche sin límites, vivimos
sin muerte, oh hermosa mía, una noche infinita.

Sobre un seno azulado reposa blandamente
mi testa fatigada del mundo. Siento sólo
tu sangre ya poblada de luces, de miriadas
de astros, y beso el pulso suave del universo y toco
tu rostro con el leve fulgor de mi mejilla.

Oh triste, oh grave noche completa. Amada, yaces
perfecta y te repaso, te ciño. Mundo solo.
Universal vivir de un cuerpo que, hecho luces,
má allá de la vida de un hombre amor permites.

Vicente Aleixandre
BEYOND

Beyond life, my love, always farther beyond,
now ethereal, unique, upon a couch of stars,
we populate the limitless night, we live
without death, oh my beauty, an infinite night.

Weary of the world my head settles
softly on a bluish breast. I sense only
your blood now peopled with lights, with myriad
stars, and I kiss the soft pulse of the universe and touch
your face with the subtle radiance of my cheek.

Oh sad, oh grave total night. Beloved, you lie
perfect and I retrace you, embrace you. Solitary world.
Universal living of a body, made into lights,
you permit love beyond the life of a man.

from *Poemas varios; 1927-1967*, 1968
P.H.

Ballads (Romances)

These are the popular songs of Old Spain whose value and beauty were recognized by the humanists, poets, and musicians of the Renaissance. The first printed collections, called *Cancioneros*, were published in the early 1500s, although the original versions may date with Spain's 12th and 13th century epic poems. Sixteenth-century Spanish artists incorporated the traditional forms and styles, the eight-syllable line and assonant rhyme, of these romances in their own work, creating new romances whose popularity has lasted.

Anónimo
LA CONSTANCIA

Mis arreos son las armas
mi descanso es pelear,
mi cama las duras peñas,
mi dormir siempre velar.
Las manidas son escuras,
los caminos por usar,
el cielo con sus mudanzas
ha por bien de me dañar,
andando de sierra en sierra
por orillas de la mar,
por probar si mi ventura
hay lugar donde avadar.
Pero por vos, mi señora,
todo se ha de comportar.

Anonymous
BALLAD OF CONSTANCY

My raiment is my weapons,
my rest is in the fray,
my bed the jagged cliffs,
my slumber to stay awake.
The haunts are all in darkness,
yet I must walk the byways,
heaven in its caprice
sees fit to cause me pain,
wandering from crag to crag,
and along the ocean's waves,
to see if my good fortune,
may cross over in some place.
But for you, my lady,
all must be braved.

Before 1500.
from *Cancionero de romances*, 1550
P.H.

Anónimo
LA LINDA AMIGA

"Compañero, compañero,
casóse mi linda amiga,
casóse con un villano
que es lo que más me dolía.
Irme quiero a tornar moro
allende la morería:
cristiano que allá pasare
yo le quitaré la vida."
"No lo hagas, compañero,
no lo hagas por tu vida,
de tres hermanas que tengo,
darte he yo la más garrida,
si la quieres por mujer,
si la quieres por amiga."
"Ni la quiero por mujer,
ni la quiero por amiga,
pues que no pude gozar
de aquélla que más quería."

Anonymous
BALLAD OF MY BEAUTIFUL LADY

"My friend, my friend,
my beautiful lady married today,
she married a country peasant,
which caused me the most pain.
I think I shall become a Moor,
and abide by Moorish ways:
any Christian that I may see,
his life I'll take away."
"Don't do it, my friend,
don't lead your life astray,
of three sisters that I have,
I shall give you the most fair,
if you want her for a wife,
if you want her for your lady."
"I don't want her for a wife,
nor want her for a lady,
since I could not enjoy,
the one I lost today."

Before 1500
from *Cancionero de romances*, 1550
P.H.

Emilio Ballagas

born in Camagüey, Cuba,
November 7, 1908

died in Havana, September 11, 1954

In his youth, Emilio Ballagas read, wrote, and dreamed of living in a place more "civilized" than his native country. After graduating from the University of Havana, he taught for nearly 13 years at a teachers' college in the provincial town of Santa Clara. He made one brief journey to Paris, where he spent four joyful months, and in 1946, after receiving a doctorate in Cuba, he won a scholarship to study in New York. There he met a Cuban student, Antonia López Villaverde, whom he married on their return to Cuba. Ballagas' work caught the exuberance of Cuba's black population. In *Júbilo y fuga* (1931), which is characterized by a quest for a "pure and refined" poetry, there are examples of Ballagas' fascination with expressive possibilities of word sounds that lead to the dominant tropical rhythms and sounds of black Cuban culture in his most popular book, *Cuaderno de poesía negra* (1934).

Emilio Ballagas
ELEGÍA DE MARÍA BELÉN CHACÓN

María Belén, María Belén, María Belén.
María Belén Chacón, María Belén Chacón,
                        María Belén Chacón,
con tus nalgas en vaivén,
de Camagüey a Santiago, de Santiago a Camagüey.

En el cielo de la rumba,
ya nunca habrá de alumbrar
tu constelación de curvas.

¿Qué ladrido te mordió el vértice del pulmón?
María Belén Chacón, María Belén Chacón...
¿Qué ladrido te mordió el vértice del pulmón?

Ni fue ladrido ni uña,
ni fue uña ni fue daño.
La plancha, de madrugada, fue quien te quemó
                        el pulmón!
María Belén Chacón, María Belén Chacón...

Y luego, por la mañana,
con la ropa, en la canasta, se llevaron tu sandunga,
tu sandunga y tu pulmón.

¡Que no baile nadie ahora!
¡Que no le arranque más pulgas el negro Andrés a su tres!

Y los chinos, que arman tánganas adentro de las maracas,
hagan un poco de paz.
Besar la cruz de las claves.
(¡Líbranos de todo mal, Virgen de la Caridad!)

Ya no veré mis instintos
en los espejos redondos y alegres de tus dos nalgas.
Tu constelación de curvas
ya no alumbrará jamás el cielo de la sandunga.

Emilio Ballagas
ELEGY FOR MARÍA BELÉN CHACÓN

María Belén, María Belén, María Belén.
María Belén Chacón, María Belén Chacón,
                    María Belén Chacón.
watching your hips roll and sway,
from Camagüey to Santiago, from Santiago to Camagüey.

Now the constellation of your curves
will never shine its light again
in rumba heaven.

What demon tore out a piece of your lung?
María Belén Chacón, María Belén Chacón...
What demon tore out a piece of your lung?

Not a demon nor a charm,
not a charm to cast the harm.
Ironing, at early dawn, hurt and burned your lung!
María Belén Chacón, María Belén Chacón...

Then, in the light of the morning,
with the basket of clothes, the lovely way you used to sway
was carried away with your lung.

No one dance here now!
And tell black André not to play his frantic music
                    for a while!
And those halfbreeds, scrapping inside the maracas,
make them hold their peace.
Just kiss the cross of the rhythm sticks.
(Pity on us Virgin of Mercy, free us from all evil!)

I'll never be able to watch again
your round and happy hips reflecting my desires.
Your constellation of curves
will never shine its light again in rumba-dancing heaven.

María Belén Chacón, María Belén Chacón.
María Belén, María Belén:
con tus nalgas en vaivén,
de Camagüey a Santiago...
de Santiago a Camagüey.

María Belén Chacón, María Belén Chacón.
María Belén, María Belén:
watching your hips roll and sway,
from Camagüey to Santiago . . .
from Santiago to Camagüey.

from *Cuaderno de poesía negra*, 1934
P.H.

Gustavo Adolfo Bécquer   *born in Seville, Spain, February 17, 1836*
died in Madrid, December 22, 1870

Gustavo Adolfo Bécquer is one of Spain's greatest 19th-century lyric poets. "Rima LIII," (Volverán las oscuras golondrinas . . . "), his most popular poem, is one of the best examples of Spanish Romanticism. His parents died when he was 10; at age 17 he followed his brother Valeriano, a painter, to Madrid, where he supported himself by journalism and hack writing. He lived a bohemian life, in complete poverty, and was chronically ill with tuberculosis. During those difficult years, he wrote haunting tales and legends, as well as the melancholic *Rimas*, which were published after his death. He fell in love with the daughter of a famous orchestra leader, but she refused him. An unhappy marriage with Casta Esteban y Navarro ended quickly, Bécquer receiving custody of their young children. He died at the age of 34; his last words to his friends were, "take care of my children."

Gustavo Adolfo Bécquer
VOLVERÁN LAS OSCURAS GOLONDRINAS...

Volverán las oscuras golondrinas
en tu balcón sus nidos a colgar,
y, otra vez, con el ala a sus cristales
jugando llamarán;

pero aquéllas que el vuelo refrenaban
tu hermosura y mi dicha a contemplar,
aquéllas que aprendieron nuestros nombres...
ésas... ¡no volverán!

Volverán las tupidas madreselvas
de tu jardín las tapias a escalar,
y otra vez a la tarde, aun más hermosas,
sus flores se abrirán;

pero aquéllas cuajadas de rocío,
cuyas gotas mirábamos temblar
y caer, como lágrimas del día...
ésas... ¡no volverán!

Volverán del amor en tus oídos
las palabras ardientes a sonar;
tu corazón de su profundo sueño
tal vez despertará;

pero mudo y absorto y de rodillas,
como se adora a Dios ante su altar,
como yo te he querido... desengáñate,
¡así no te querrán!

Gustavo Adolfo Bécquer
THE DARK-WINGED SWALLOWS WILL RETURN...

The dark-winged swallows will return
to hang their nests beneath your eaves,
and before your windows once again
beckon with their wings;

but those who flight restrained
your beauty and my joy to learn,
those who came to know our names...
those... will not return!

The twining honeysuckles will return
your garden walls to climb
and on another afternoon, more lovely still,
again their flowers will bloom;

but those with sparkling drops of dew,
which we'd watch trembling, yearn
and fall, like teardrops of the day...
those... will not return!

From love will come once more the sound
of burning words to ring;
your heart from within its soundest sleep
perhaps will rise again;

but mute, entranced and kneeling down
as adoring God before His throne,
as I have loved you... accept the truth!
they will not love you so!

from *Rimas*, 1871
P.H.

45

Jorge Luis Borges

born in Buenos Aires, Argentina, August 24, 1899

died in Buenos Aires, June 14, 1986

Jorge Luis Borges is the foremost Spanish American writer of short stories, essays and poetry. He is known for his labyrinthine weaving of cultures, concepts, and time. He has also created captivatingly beautiful images which express moments of profound comprehension and intimate feeling. He learned English from his English grandmother, and then mastered many other languages. His family moved to Switzerland in 1914, where he attended school; he returned permanently to Argentina in 1921. Borges' father and his paternal grandmother became blind in adulthood. After an accident much like that of the main character in his famous short story, *El Sur* (*The South*), Borges' eyesight grew worse; he has been completely blind since the 1960s. During the 1940s, Borges fell into disfavor with Juan Perón, who removed him as director of the National Library and made him a government inspector of poultry. However, he published many of his best short stories then. After Perón fell in 1955, Borges returned to his library position and rose to international literary eminence.

Jorge Luis Borges
AMOROSA ANTICIPACIÓN

Ni la intimidad de tu frente clara como una fiesta
ni la privanza de tu cuerpo, aún misterioso y tácito
                                y de niña,
ni la sucesión de tu vida situándose en palabras
                                o acallamiento
serán favor tan misterioso
como el mirar tu sueño implicado
en la vigilia de mis brazos.
Virgen milagrosamente otra vez por la virtud absolutoria
                                del sueño,
quieta y resplandeciente como una dicha en la selección
                                del recuerdo,
me darás esa orilla de tu vida que tú misma no tienes.
Arrojado a quietud,
divisaré esa playa última de tu ser
y te veré por vez primera, quizá,
como Dios ha de verte,
desbaratada la ficción del Tiempo,
sin el amor, sin mí.

Jorge Luis Borges
AMOROUS ANTICIPATION

Not the intimacy of your forehead clear as a celebration
nor the prize of your body, still mysterious and tacit
                                   and childlike
nor the sequence of your life showing itself in words
                                   or silence
will be so mysterious a favor
as to watch your dream implied
in the vigil of my arms.
Miraculously virgin again through the absolving virtue of sleep,
quiet and resplendent like a lucky choice of memories,
you will give me those far reaches of your life that you yourself
                                   do not have.
Cast into stillness,
I will perceive that ultimate strand of your being
and will see you for the first time, perhaps
as God must see you,
the fiction of Time destroyed,
without love, without me.

from *Luna de enfrente*, 1925
P.H.

49

Luis Cernuda

born in Seville, Spain,
September 21, 1902

died in Mexico City, Mexico,
October 5, 1963

At the University of Seville, Cernuda was led to French literature by a professor, the poet Pedro Salinas, who was to become a close friend. While Cernuda's poetry is indelibly marked by French surrealism, his imagery never becomes extreme. Frequently the theme of his poems is love touched by other love, with a quest for the physical ideal. Integrating his personal history into his poetry, Cernuda wrote erotic poems once considered scandalous because of their homosexual content. Outspoken in his support of the Republican cause during the Spanish civil war, he was never able to return to his country. After teaching in England, Scotland, and the United States, he moved permanently to Mexico in 1952.

Luis Cernuda
UNOS CUERPOS SON COMO FLORES…

Unos cuerpos son como flores,
Otros como puñales,
Otros como cintas de agua;
Pero todos, temprano o tarde,
Serán quemaduras que en otro cuerpo se agranden,
Convirtiendo por virtud del fuego a una piedra
en un hombre.

Pero el hombre se agita en todas direcciones,
Sueña con libertades, compite con el viento,
Hasta que un día la quemadura se borra,
Volviendo a ser piedra en el camino de nadie.

Yo, que no soy piedra, sino camino
Que cruzan al pasar los pies desnudos,
Muero de amor por todos ellos;
Les doy mi cuerpo para que lo pisen,
Aunque les lleve a una ambición o a una nube,
Sin que ninguno comprenda
Que ambiciones o nubes
No valen un amor que se entrega.

Luis Cernuda
SOME BODIES ARE LIKE FLOWERS...

Some bodies are like flowers,
others like knives,
others like ribbons of water;
but all of them, sooner or later,
will be burns that spread on another body,
the power of fire turning a stone into a man.

But man grows aimlessly restless,
he dreams of liberties, he challenges the wind
until one day the burn is gone,
changing back into a stone that lies in no one's way.

I, I am not a stone, but a pathway
crisscrossed by naked feet.
I am dying of love for them all;
my body is theirs to walk on,
though it lead them to ambition or to a cloud,
without one of them realizing
that ambitions or clouds
are not worth a willing love.

from *Los placeres prohibidos*, 1931
P.H.

Rubén Darío

born Félix Rubén García Sarmiento, in Metapa, Nicaragua, January 18, 1867

died in León, Nicaragua, February 6, 1916

Rubén Darío revolutionized Spanish and Spanish American literature with his *Azul* (1888), published when he was only 21. His poems and short stories show influence of the French romantics, Parnassians and decadents, and the Spanish baroque poets, all combined in an original, exuberant, melodious and highly refined style which breathed new life into Hispanic letters. He never knew his real parents, who had separated before he was born. He was raised by godparents in Léon, and at 13, some of his verses were published in the city newspaper. At 14, he decided to marry, but considering it folly, his friends collected money to send him to El Salvador. Thus began a bohemian life in the Americas and Europe. He counted many women among his friends, and married several times. According to Darío's biographers, he was a timid, homely man—yet his name is synonymous with the lavish literary elegance called *Modernismo* of which he was leader and foremost poet.

Rubén Darío
ERA UN AIRE SUAVE...

Era un aire suave, de pausados giros;
el hada Harmonía ritmaba sus vuelos;
e iban frases vagas y tenues suspiros
entre los sollozos de los violoncelos.

Sobre la terraza junto a los ramajes,
diríase un trémolo de liras eolias
cuando acariciaban los sedosos trajes
sobre el tallo erguidas las blancas magnolias.

La marquesa Eulalia risas y desvíos
daba a un tiempo mismo para dos rivales:
el vizconde rubio de los desafíos
y el abate joven de los madrigales.

Cerca, coronado con hojas de viña,
reía en su máscara Término barbudo,
y, como un efebo que fuese una niña,
mostraba una Diana su mármol desnudo.

Y bajo un boscaje del amor palestra,
sobre rico zócalo al modo de Jonia,
con un candelabro prendido en la diestra
volaba el Mercurio de Juan de Bolonia.

La orquesta perlaba sus mágicas notas;
un coro de sones alados se oía;
galantes pavanas, fugaces gavotas
cantaban los dulces violines de Hungría.

Al oír las quejas de sus caballeros,
ríe, ríe, ríe la divina Eulalia,
pues son su tesoro las flechas de Eros
el cinto de Cipria, la rueca de Onfalia.

Rubén Darío
IT WAS A GENTLE AIR...

It was a gentle air of lilting spirals;
the Fairy Harmony paced his melodies;
and faint phrases and sighs went floating away
among the sobbing sounds of the violincellos.

Near the foliage, upon the terrace,
it might have been called a tremolo of lyres of Aeolus
when silken gowns were caressed
beside stiff stems of white magnolias.

The Marquise Eulalie, was laughing and cruel
at the same time to two rivals:
the fairhaired viscount of the duels
and the young abbot of the madrigals.

Nearby, crowned with leaves of the vine,
bearded Terminus laughed in his mask,
and, like a girlish young man,
a Diana showed her marble nakedness.

And beneath a bower of palaestrian love,
upon a luxurious socle in the style of Ionia,
a candleabrum held in his right hand above,
flew the Mercury of Giovanni di Bologna.

The orchestra purled its magical notes;
a chorus of winged sounds were heard;
gallant pavans and fleeting gavottes,
the sweet violins of Hungary stirred.

Hearing the plaints of her two caballeros,
Divine Eulalie laughs and laughs and laughs,
for her treasures are the arrows of Eros,
the Cyprian belt, and Omphale's distaff.

¡Ay de quien sus mieles y frases recoja!
¡Ay de quien del canto de su amor se fíe!
Con sus ojos lindos y su boca roja,
La divina Eulalia ríe, ríe, ríe.

Tiene azules ojos, es maligna y bella;
cuando mira, vierte viva luz extraña:
se asoma a sus húmedas pupilas de estrella
el alma del rubio cristal de Champaña.

Es noche de fiesta, y el baile de trajes
ostenta su gloria de triunfos mundanos.
La divina Eulalia, vestida de encajes,
una flor destroza con sus tersas manos.

El teclado armónico de su risa fina
a la alegre música de un pájaro iguala,
con los staccati de una bailarina
y las locas fugas de una colegiala.

¡Amoroso pájaro que trinos exhala
bajo el ala a veces ocultando el pico;
que desdenes rudos lanza bajo el ala,
bajo el ala aleve del leve abanico!

Cuando a media noche sus notas arranque
y en arpegios áureos gima Filomela,
y el ebúrneo cisne, sobre el quieto estanque,
como blanca góndola imprima su estela,

la marquesa alegre llegará al boscaje,
boscaje que cubre la amable glorieta
donde han de estrecharla los brazos de un paje,
que siendo su paje será su poeta.

Al compás de un canto de artista de Italia
que en la brisa errante la orquesta deslíe,
junto a los rivales, la divina Eulalia,
la divina Eulalie ríe, ríe, ríe.

Woe is he who partakes of her honey and phrases!
Woe is he who puts faith in her songs of love!
With her mouth of red and her beautiful eyes,
Divine Eulalie laughs, laughs and laughs.

She has eyes of blue, she is lovely and evil,
in her eyes shines an eerie bright flame;
and flowing from her moist starlike pupils
is the soul of the fair crystal of Champagne.

It is the night of the ball, and the masquerade
flaunts the glory of worldly man.
Divine Eulalie, dressed up in lace,
crushes a flower with her polished hands.

The harmonious keyboard of her delicate laughter
the joyous music of a bird equates
to the staccati steps of a ballerina
and a schoolgirl's childish and crazy flights.

Amorous bird, trills exhaling,
hiding her beak beneath her hand;
who launches such scorn beneath her wing,
beneath the perfidious wing of her feathered fan!

When midnight comes and her notes begin
and in golden arpeggios Philomela complains,
and the ivory swan, on the glassy lagoon,
like a white gondola will etch his wake,

the merry Marquise will come to the foliage,
the foliage that covers the amiable bower
where there will embrace her the arms of a page,
who being a page will be her poet.

To the pulse of a song by an artist of Italy
which into the errant breeze the orchestra wafts,
beside her two rivals, Divine Eulalie,
Divine Eulalie laughs, laughs and laughs.

¿Fue acaso en el tiempo del rey Luis de Francia,
sol con corte de astros, en campo de azur
cuando los alcázares llenó de fragancia
la regia y pomposa rosa Pompadour?

¿Fue cuando la bella su falda cogía
con dedos de ninfa, bailando el minué,
y de los compases el ritmo seguía
sobre el tacón rojo, lindo y leve pie?

¿O cuando pastoras de floridos valles
ornaban con cintas sus albos corderos,
y oían, divinas Tirsis de Versalles,
las declaraciones de sus caballeros?

¿Fue en ese buen tiempo de duques pastores,
de amantes princesas y tiernos galanes,
cuando entre sonrisas y perlas y flores
iban las casacas de los chambelanes?

¿Fue acaso en el Norte o en el Mediodía?
Yo el tiempo y el día y el país ignoro,
pero sé que Eulalia ríe todavía,
¡y es crüel y eterna su risa de oro!

Was it the time perchance of King Louis of France,
a sun with a court of stars, on a field of azure,
when the palaces were filled with fragrance
by the pompous and regal rose Pompadour?

Was when the beauty herself lifted her dress,
with the fingers of a nymph, dancing the minuet,
and then followed the pulsating musical stress
with red heels and her light pretty foot?

Or when shepherdesses from flowery valleys
bedecked with bows their snowy lambs,
and heard, divine Thyrsis of Versailles,
the vows of love from their gentlemen?

Was it in those good times of shepherd-dukes,
of princess-lovers and tender gentlemen,
when among smiles and pearls and flowers
glided the cassocks of the chamberlains?

Was it in Northern climes or in the land of the sun?
The time and day and place I don't know,
but I know that Eulalie laughs on and on,
and cruel and eternal is her laughter of gold!

from *Prosas profanas y otros poemas*, 1896
P.H

Rubén Darío
¡CARNE, CELESTE
CARNE DE LA MUJER!...

¡Carne, celeste carne de la mujer! Arcilla
—dijo Hugo—; ambrosía más bien, ¡oh maravilla!
La vida se soporta,
tan doliente y tan corta,
solamente por eso:
roce, mordisco o beso
en ese pan divino
para el cual nuestra sangre es nuestro vino.
En ella está la lira,
en ella está la rosa,
en ella está la ciencia armonïosa,
en ella se respira
el perfume vital de toda cosa.

Eva y Cipris concentran el misterio
del corazón del mundo.
Cuando el áureo Pegaso
en la victoria matinal se lanza
con el mágico ritmo de su paso
hacia la vida y hacia la esperanza,
si alza la crin y las narices hincha
y sobre las montañas pone el casco sonoro
y hacia la mar relincha,
y el espacio se llena
de un gran temblor de oro,
es que ha visto desnuda a Anadiomena.

Gloria, ¡Oh Potente a quien las sombras temen!
¡Que las más blancas tórtolas te inmolen!
¡Pues por ti la floresta está en el polen
y el pensamiento en el sagrado semen!

Gloria, ¡oh Sublime, que eres la existencia
por quien siempre hay futuros en el útero eterno!
¡Tu boca sabe al fruto del árbol de la Ciencia,
y al torcer tus cabellos apagaste el infierno!

Rubén Darío

FLESH, CELESTIAL
FLESH OF WOMAN!...

Flesh, celestial flesh of woman! Clay
—said Hugo—; ambrosia, better said,—how marvelous!
We bear life,
so painful and so short,
only for that:
caress, nibble or kiss
on that divine bread
for which our blood is our wine.
In her is the lyre,
in her is the rose,
in her is the harmonious science,
in her we breathe
the vital perfume of all things.

Eve and Cypris concentrate the mystery
of the heart of the world.
When golden Pegasus
rushes into the morning victory
with the magical rhythm of his step
toward life and toward hope,
if he arches his mane and his nostrils swell
and he gallops the mountains with sonorous hoof
and he neighs out toward the open sea,
and space is filled
with a great trembling of gold...
it is all for having seen Anadyomene naked.

Glory! oh Power whom shadows fear!
May the white doves immolate you!
For because of you the forest lives in the pollen
and thought in the sacred semen!

Glory! oh Sublime, for you are the existence
whereby futures exist forever in the eternal womb!
Your mouth tastes of the fruit of the tree of Science,
and with a twist of your hair you extinguished Hell!

Inútil es el grito de la legión cobarde
del interés, inútil el progreso
yanqui si te desdeña.
Si el progreso es de fuego, por ti arde.
¡Toda lucha del hombre va a tu beso,
por ti se combate o se sueña!

Pues en ti existe Primavera para el triste,
labor gozosa para el fuerte,
néctar, ánfora, dulzura amable.
¡Porque en ti existe
el placer de vivir hasta la muerte
y ante la eternidad de lo probable...!

Useless is the cry of the cowardly legion
of self interest, useless the progress
of the Yankee if he disdains you.
If progress is fire, it burns for you.
Every human struggle is for your kiss,
for you we fight or dream!

For in you is Spring for those who are sad,
joyous labor for the strong,
nectar, amphora, gentle sweetness.
For in you exists
the pleasure of living until death
before the eternity of what probably is . . . !

from *Cantos de vida y esperanza*, 1905
P.H.

Baldomero Fernández Moreno   *born in Buenos Aires, Argentina,*
                                    November 15, 1886

                                    died in Buenos Aires, July 7, 1950

Baldomero Fernández Moreno's poems celebrate the simple beauty of
family life in the Argentine countryside. His parents were Spanish,
and they took him to Santander, where he spent his early childhood.
After returning to Buenos Aires, he chose medicine as his profession.
His first book of poems, *Las iniciales del misal,* was published in
1915, and he gave up medicine in 1924 to write and teach. He
published five books in the 1920s and 1930s, won two literary prizes,
and was appointed to the Argentine Academy of Letters in 1934. After
one of his sons died in 1937, Fernández Moreno had a nervous
breakdown but continued writing, and although his poetry became
filled with a sense of death he never abandoned his vision of ordinary
Argentine life.

Baldomero Fernández Moreno
HABLA LA MADRE CASTELLANA

Estos hijos—dice ella,
la madre dulce y santa—,
estos hijos tan desobedientes
que a lo mejor contestan una mala palabra...

En el regazo tiene
un montón de tiernísimas chauchas
que va quebrando lentamente
y echando en una cacerola con agua.

—¡Cómo os acordaréis
cuando ya esté enterrada!—
Tenemos en los ojos
y la ocultamos, una lágrima.

Silencio.
Al quebrarse las chauchas
hacen entre sus dedos
una detonación menudita y simpática.

Baldomero Fernández Moreno
THE CASTILLIAN MOTHER SPEAKS

These children nowadays—she says,
sweet and blessed mother—,
these children are so unruly
likely as not they'll just talk back to me . . .

Oh her lap she has
a pile of green beans fresh from the garden
that she is methodically breaking
and dropping into a pan of water.

—I'm sure you'll remember me
when I'm dead and gone!—
we have in our eyes
but we hide them, tears.

Silence.
As she is breaking the green beans
between her fingers they are making
a quiet, pleasant popping.

from *Poesía*, 1928
P.H.

Garcilaso de la Vega

born in Toledo, Spain , ca. 1503

died in Nice, France, October 14, 1536

Garcilaso de la Vega is known for having introduced Italian Renaissance forms and themes into Spanish literature, and for beautifully controlled verses that express profound emotion. Garcilaso was an ideal courtier of Spain's Golden Age, excelling both in literature and in military pursuits. At 17, he joined the court of the Emperor, Charles V. When the Turks beseiged Vienna in 1529, Garcilaso volunteered. After he displeased the Emperor, he was imprisoned on an island in the Danube, until given the choice of entering a monastery or serving Charles in Naples. He chose the latter, and lived a sumptuous life in literary and social circles. On a French campaign near Cannes, Garcilaso led an assault up a fortress wall and was severely wounded when French gunners dropped a rock on him. He was taken to Nice and died there 18 days later. His few poems, unpublished during his life, were preserved by his friend Juan Boscán.

Garcilaso de la Vega
¡OH DULCES PRENDAS...

¡Oh dulces prendas, por mi mal halladas,
dulces y alegres cuando Dios quería!
Juntas estáis en la memoria mía,
y con ella en mi muerte conjuradas.

¡Quién me dijera, cuando en las pasadas
horas en tanto bien por vos me vía,
que me habíades de ser en algún día
con tan grave dolor representadas?

Pues en una hora junto me llevastes
todo el bien que por términos me distes,
llevadme junto el mal que me dejastes.

Si no, sospecharé que me pusistes
en tantos bienes, porque deseastes
verme morir entre memorias tristes.

Garcilaso de la Vega
OH SWEET SOUVENIRS...

Oh sweet souvenirs, through my misfortune found,
sweet and happy when God so willed it!
You are together in my memory bound,
and with it have conspired my death.

Who could ever know, when in the past
hours in such joy from you I seemed,
that you would to me some day at last,
in such painful grief be seen.

Since in one single hour from me you stole
all the pleasures you had timely given me,
take from me now the evil left as well.

If not, I will suspect that you bestowed
on me such treasures, because you wished to see
me die among sad memories.

1534
from *Obras*, 1924
P.H.

Luis de Góngora y Argote

born in Córdoba, Spain, July 11, 1561
died in Córdoba, May 23, 1627

Although Góngora's first poems were written in the balanced, harmonious style of the Renaissance, they already showed signs of the extreme elaboration of images and language which was to become known as Gongorismo and would become definitive of Spanish baroque poetry. Often in Góngora's poems complex images of physical beauty mask a disordered void, or fade rapidly into nothingness.

Góngora came from a high-born family and was educated at the famous University of Salamanca, but he did not receive an appointment to court as was expected. His bishop wrote: "He rarely attends church, and when he does he prays with little devotion; he frequents the bullfights, runs around day and night with actors, and writes profane verses." However, in 1606, he finally acquired an "honorary chaplaincy" in the court of Philip III, and in 1617 he became a priest. Immensely popular, Góngora was at the center of controversy, particularly because of the literary salvos exchanged with the other great Spanish poets of the day, Lope de Vega and Francisco de Quevedo, who criticized his tortuous syntax, latinized vocabulary, and mythological allusions.

Luis de Góngora y Argote
MIENTRAS POR COMPETIR
CON TU CABELLO...

Mientras por competir con tu cabello,
oro bruñido al sol relumbra en vano;
mientras con menosprecio en medio el llano
mira tu blanca frente el lilio bello;

mientras a cada labio, por cogello,
siguen más ojos que al clavel temprano,
y mientras triunfa con desdén lozano
del luciente cristal tu gentil cuello;

goza cuello, cabello, labio y frente,
antes que lo que fue en tu edad dorada
oro, lirio, clavel, cristal luciente,

no sólo en plata o vïola troncada
se vuelva, mas tú y ello juntamente
en tierra, en polvo, en humo, en sombra, en nada.

Luis de Góngora y Argote
WHILE TRYING TO RIVAL
YOUR HAIR...

While trying to rival your hair,
burnished gold in the sun shines in vain;
while disdainful in midst of the plain,
you observe the pale lily with forehead fair;

while watching your lips, trying to take them,
are more eyes than following fresh carnations,
and while standing in haughty triumph
of glittering crystal is your elegant neck;

enjoy neck, hair, forehead and lips,
before that which was in your golden age
gold, lily, carnation, and crystal aglow,

not only into silver or cut violet
changes, but you and it together all
into dirt, into smoke, into dust, into darkness,
into nothingness.

1582
from *Obras completas*, 1967
P.H.

Luis de Góngora y Argote
LA DULCE BOCA...

La dulce boca que a gustar convida
un humor entre perlas destilado,
y a no invidiar aquel licor sagrado
que a Júpiter ministra el garzón de Ida,

amantes, no toquéis, si queréis vida;
porque entre un labio y otro colorado
Amor está, de su veneno armado,
cual entre flor y flor sierpe escondida.

No os engañen las rosas que a la Aurora
diréis que, aljofaradas y olorosas,
se le cayeron del purpúreo seno.

¡Manzanas son de Tántalo, y no rosas,
que después huyen del que incitan ahora,
y sólo del Amor queda el veneno!

Luis de Góngora y Argote
THE SWEET MOUTH ...

The sweet mouth that is inviting to taste
a humor distilled among pearls,
and to envy not that nectar of gods
which young Ida to Jupiter takes,

lovers do not touch, if you wish life:
for between one lip and the other of red
is Love, with its venom armed
as between flower and flower a serpent lies.

Do not be deceived by the roses in the Aurora
which you believe, pearled with dew and sweet of scent,
fell to you from the purple bosom.

Apples of Tantalus they are, and not roses,
which later flee from the one they now tempt,
and all that remains of Love is venom.

1584
from *Obras completas*, 1967
P.H.

Jorge Guillén   *born in Valladolid, Spain,*
                       January 18, 1893

                       died in Madrid, February 6, 1984

Jorge Guillén is of the school of "pure" poets like Juan Ramón
Jiménez who attempt to refine word and image to their most
expressive state. In Guillén's case the result is poems with an
essentially positive view of life and love, characterized by tremendous
economy of words, and clear, precise images often requiring
considerable contemplation to comprehend. In addition to being a
distinguished poet, he was a professor of literature at many
prestigious universities in Europe and the Americas. At the
Sorbonne, early in his career, he married Germaine Cohen. At the
outbreak of the Spanish civil war in 1936, Guillén was detained in
Pamplona by Franquistas as a known supporter of the Republic, but
he was permitted to immigrate with his family to the United States.
When Franco died in 1975, he returned to Spain and lived in Málaga.

Jorge Guillén
LOS FIELES AMANTES

Noche mucho más noche: el amor ya es un hecho.
Feliz nivel de paz extiende el sueño
Como una perfección todavía amorosa.
Bulto adorable, lejos
Ya, se adormece,
Y a su candor en isla se abandona,
Animal por ahí, latente.
¡Qué diario Infinito sobre el lecho
De una pasión: costumbre rodeada de arcano!
¡Oh noche, más oscura en nuestros brazos!

Jorge Guillén
THE FAITHFUL LOVERS

Night, more night: love now a fact.
Joyful level of peace extends the dream
Like a perfection loving yet.
Beloved form, far off
Now, falling asleep,
And yields to its purity in isolation,
The animal somewhere there, latent.
Such daily infinity upon the bed
Of passion: custom surrounded by enigma!
Oh night, darker in our arms!

from *Cántico*; *1919-1950*, 1950
P.H.

Jorge Guillén
CIMA DE LA DELICIA

¡Cima de la delicia!
Todo en el aire es pájaro.
Se cierne lo inmediato
Resuelto en lejanía.

¡Hueste de esbeltas fuerzas!
¡Qué alacridad de mozo
En el espacio airoso,
Henchido de presencia!

El mundo tiene cándida
Profundidad de espejo.
Las más claras distancias
Sueñan lo verdadero.

¡Dulzura de los años
Irreparables! ¡Bodas
Tardías con la historia
Que desamé a diario!

Más, todavía más.
Hacia el sol, en volandas
La plenitud se escapa.
¡Ya sólo sé cantar!

Jorge Guillén
SUMMIT OF DELIGHT

Summit of delight!
Everything in the air is bird.
The immediate hovers
Resolute on the distance.

Host of slender forces!
What youthful alacrity
In the airy space,
Swollen with presence!

The world has the candid
Depth of a mirror.
The clearest distances
Dream what is true.

Sweetness of the years
We cannot retrieve! Belated marriage
With that history
I ceased loving each day!

More, still more.
Toward the sun, taking flight
Plenitude escapes.
Now I only can sing!

from *Cántico; 1919-1950*, 1950
P.H.

Nicolás Guillén   *born in Camagüey, Cuba, July 10, 1902*

Nicolás Guillén's first poems showed strong influence of the exotic
world of the Spanish American Modernists, but his work soon
evolved to a more immediate expression of Cuban life. His poems
written in the language and rhythm of Cuba's poor blacks are his
most popular and he is known as a leading exponent of
Afro-Antillean "poesía negra" along with Luis Palés Matos and
Emilio Ballagas. Later he moved to wider political and social themes
in his *Cantos para soldados y Sones para turistas* (1937) and in *La
paloma del vuelo popular* (1958). Guillén has been a life-long
revolutionary activist in Cuba, as was his father (who died in the 1917
revolution against Mario García Menocal's regime). Jailed in 1936 for
publishing "subversive material," and released in 1937, he went to
wartime Spain to participate in the International Congress for the
Defense of Culture. He was exiled from Cuba by the Batista
government in 1953 for his rebellious activities, and spent the years
until Castro's triumph in 1959, in Buenos Aires. Since 1961 he has
been the president of the Writers and Artists Union of Cuba.

Nicolás Guillén
BÚCATE PLATA

Búcate plata,
búcate plata,
porque no doy un paso má:
etoy a arró con galleta
na má.

Yo bien sé cómo etá to,
pero viejo, hay que comer;
búcate plata,
búcate plata,
porque me voy a correr.

Depué dirán que soy mala,
y no me querrán tratar,
pero amor con hambre, viejo,
¡qué va!
Con tanto zapato nuevo,
¡qué va!
Con tanto reló, compadre,
¡qué va!
Con tanto lujo, mi negro,
¡qué va!

Nicolás Guillén
GO GET SOME BREAD

Go get some bread,
go get some bread,
or I'm not going another step:
I'm up to here with rice and crackers
nothing else.

I know how tough things are,
but man, but we got to eat:
go get some bread,
go get some bread,
or I'm going to split.

I know they'll say I'm no good,
and won't want to see me no more,
but making love when you're hungry, man,
is no good at all!
with all those new shoes out there,
it's no good at all!
with all those watches out there, love,
it's no good at all!
with all those fine things out there, you black bum,
it's no good at all!

from *Motivos de son*, 1930
P.H.

Nicolás Guillén
BARES

Amo los bares y tabernas
junto al mar,
donde la gente charla y bebe
sólo por beber y charlar.
Donde Juan Nadie llega y pide
su trago elemental,
y están Juan Bronco y Juan Navaja
y Juan Narices y hasta Juan Simple,
el sólo, el simplemente Juan.

Allí la blanca ola
bate de la amistad;
una amistad de pueblo, sin retórica,
una ola de ¡hola! ¿cómo estás?
Allí huele a pescado,
a mangle, a ron, a sal
y a camisa sudada puesta a secar al sol.

Búscame, hermano, y me hallarás
(en La Habana, en Oporto,
en Jacmel, en Shanghai)
con la sencilla gente
que sólo por beber y charlar
puebla los bares y tabernas
junto al mar.

Nicolás Guillén
BARS

I love bars and taverns
beside the sea,
where people talk and drink
just to drink and talk.
Where Joe Nobody comes in and asks for
his drink straight,
and there are Joe Brawl and Joe Blade
and Joe Blow and even Simple Joe,
just plain old Joe.

There white waves
break in friendship;
a friendship of the people, without rhetoric,
a wave of "hello!" and "how are you doing?"
There it smells of fish,
of mangrove, of rum, of salt
and of a sweaty shirt put in the sun to dry.

Look me up, brother, and you'll find me
(in Havana, in Oporto,
in Jacmel, in Shanghai)
with plain folk
who just to drink and talk
people the bars and taverns
beside the sea.

from *La paloma de vuelo popular*, 1958
P.H.

91

Miguel Hernández

born in Orihuela, Alicante, Spain,
October 30, 1910

died in Alicante, March 28, 1942

Miguel Hernández combines the style of the Spanish classics, particularly Góngora, with surreal imagery in an exceedingly personal poetry marked by intense emotion. He left school at 15 to herd his father's goats, then left Orihuela in 1932 for Madrid, where he became part of a circle of great poets, including Vicente Aleixandre and Pablo Neruda. In 1936, Hernández enlisted with Republican forces. The next year he married Josefina Manresa, and while he was at the front in Teruel, a son was born to them, but the child died before his father saw him. At the end of the war Hernández fled to Portugal, but was extradited to Spain where he was imprisoned and tortured. When freed from prison, he went home rather than make another attempt to flee the country as did other artists who fought against Franco. He was sent back to jail and sentenced to death in 1940. His sentence was then commuted to 30 years, and he died in prison in 1942. He was 31 years old.

Miguel Hernández
CANTAR

Es la casa un palomar
y la cama un jazminero.
Las puertas de par en par
y en el fondo el mundo entero.

El hijo, tu corazón
madre que se ha engrandecido.
Dentro de la habitación
todo lo que ha florecido.

El hijo te hace un jardín,
y tú has hecho al hijo, esposa,
la habitación del jazmín,
el palomar de la rosa.

Alrededor de tu piel
ato y desato la mía.
Un mediodía de miel
rezumas: un mediodía.

¿Quién en esta casa entró
y la apartó del desierto?
Para que me acuerde yo
alguien que soy yo y ha muerto.

Viene la luz más redonda
a los almendros más blancos.
La vida, la luz, se ahonda
entre muertos y barrancos.

Venturoso es el futuro,
como aquellos horizontes
de pórfido y mármol puro
donde respiran los montes.

Miguel Hernández
SONG

The house is a cote for doves
and the bed a jasmine garden.
Deep within, the entire world,
and its doors are standing open.

Our son, your heart
Oh mother big with child.
Within the dwelling
all things have come to bloom.

The child makes you a garden,
and you have made our child, my love,
a growing place for jasmine,
the dove cote of a rose.

All around your skin
I bind and unbind mine,
A noontime of honey
you exude: a noontime.

Who is it came into this house
and took it from the barren shore?
So that I remember
someone I am who is no more.

The fullest light reaches
the whitest almond trees.
Life, and light, grow deeper
among the dead and the ravines.

The future is fortunate,
like those far horizons
of pure marble and porphyry
where mountains lie breathing.

Arde la casa encendida
de besos y sombra amante.
No puede pasar la vida
más honda y emocionante.

Desbordadamente sorda
la leche alumbra tus huesos.
Y la casa se desborda
con ella, el hijo y los besos.

Tú, tu vientre caudaloso,
el hijo y el palomar.
Esposa, sobre tu esposo
suenan los pasos del mar.

The house aglow is kindled
with kisses and loving shadows.
A life cannot be lived,
deeper and more impassioned.

Overwhelmingly hushed
the milk illumines your bones.
And the home is brimming
with it, our kisses and our son.

You, your bountiful womb,
the dovecot and our son.
My wife, upon your husband
the rhythms of the sea resound.

from *Obra escogida*, 1952
P.H.

Miguel Hernández
EL AMOR ASCENDÍA
ENTRE NOSOTROS...

El amor ascendía entre nosotros
como la luna entre las dos palmeras
que nunca se abrazaron.

El íntimo rumor de los dos cuerpos
hacia el arrullo un oleaje trajo,
pero la ronca voz fué atenazada.
Fueron pétreos los labios.

El ansia de ceñir movió la carne,
esclareció los huesos inflamados,
pero los brazos al querer tenderse
murieron en los brazos.

Pasó el amor, la luna, entre nosotros
y devoró los cuerpos solitarios.
Y somos dos fantasmas que se buscan
y se encuentran lejanos.

Miguel Hernández
LOVE WAS RISING BETWEEN US...

Love was rising between us
like the moon between the two palm trees
that never embraced.

The intimate rustling of the two bodies
brought a ground-swell to the wooing,
but the husky voice was stifled.
The lips turned to stone.

The urge to join moved the flesh,
lit up the enflamed bones,
but arms reaching for
arms died.

Love, the moon, passed between us
and devoured our solitary bodies.
And we are two phantoms seeking each other,
and finding each other distant.

from *Obra escogida*, 1952
P.H.

Juana de Ibarbourou   *born in Melo, Uruguay, March 8, 1895*

died in Montevideo, Uruguay, 1979

Juana de Ibarbourou's poetry is a vital, uninhibited expression of a
woman in love. Poetry was always the passion of Juana Fernández
Morales—even as a child. At 20, the beautiful Juana married Lucas
de Ibarbourou, an army captain; they moved around the country
with his various military assignments until settling in Montevideo in
1918. Ibarbourou's exuberantly sensual poetry was spectacularly
popular throughout Latin America; and in 1929, she was feted as
"Juana de América" in a gala celebration in Montevideo, an event
attended by the great poets and artists of the time. Her husband's
death in 1942 was a great blow. The poetry of her later years becomes
nostalgic in nature and often contrasts images of old age and death
with the joyous prime of life that has passed.

Juana de Ibarbourou
MADRUGADA

He pasado la noche inquieta y desvelada.
Aclara el día y me escurro de la cama, aburrida.
Hoy yo sola paseo por esta calle extrema
de portones cerrados y de casas dormidas.

Amanecer como de humo.
Parece que el sol, malhumorado,
con leña verde preparara el fuego
para cocer su desayuno.

El viento es húmedo como recién salido
de un baño. En el cielo pálido,
las estrellas descoloridas
poco a poco se van borrando.

Pasa un lechero con boina roja.
Desde lo alto de un viejo muro,
me tienta un gajo curvo y felposo,
lleno de nísperos maduros.

Ando, ando, ando, ando.
Cuando retorne y hacia él me incline
con un beso, para despertarlo,
él pensará también, con gozo ávido,
que acabo de salir del baño.

Juana de Ibarbourou
DAWN

I have spent a restless and sleepless night.
Day is dawning and I slip out of bed, bored.
Today I alone walk along this long street
of sealed doors and sleeping houses.

A dawn like smoke.
It seems the sun, ill-humored,
has lit a fire with green wood
to cook its breakfast.

The wind is moist like it just came from
a bath. In the pale sky,
the colorless stars
little by little are vanishing.

A milkman in a red beret goes by.
From atop an old wall,
I am tempted by a bent, plush branch
heavy with ripe medlars.

I walk, walk, walk, walk.
When I return and bend over him
With a kiss, to wake him,
He will think, with hungry joy,
That I too have just come from the bath.

from *Raíz salvaje*, 1922
P.H.

Juana de Ibarbourou
LA CARICIA

La tarde taciturna se borraba
en medio de una calma dulce y quieta,
y entre la sombra azul de la glorieta
el palor de la luna se filtraba.

Tu mano, toda nervios, deshojaba
las flores de un rosal con una inquieta
impaciencia, que a veces la secreta
impulsión de un deseo apresuraba.

Y al cortar una rosa blanca y suave,
que era como una palpitante ave
que el azar en tu mano hubiera preso,

con paso cauteloso te acercaste.
Por los ojos la rosa me pasaste
y yo sentí la sensación de un beso.

Juana de Ibarbourou
THE CARESS

The soundless dusk was growing dim
in the midst of a sweet and quiet repose,
and in the blue shadows of the bower
the pallor of moonlight filtered down.

Your hand, all nerves, was stripping
petals from the roses with restless
impatience, which at times the secret
impulse of a desire was urging.

And when you'd picked a white and tender rose,
that was like a trembling bird
caught in your hand by chance,

with cautious step you drew near.
You gave me the rose with your eyes
and I felt the sensation of a kiss.

from *Las lenguas del diamante*, 1919
P.H.

Juana de Ibarbourou
TIEMPO

Me enfrento a ti, oh vida sin espigas,
desde la casa de mi soledad.
Detrás de mí anclado está aquel tiempo
en que tuve pasión y libertad,
garganta libre al amoroso grito,
y casta desnudez, y claridad.

Era una flor, oh vida, y en mí estaba
arrulladora, la eternidad.

Sombras ahora, sombras sobre el tallo,
y no sentir ya nada más
en la cegada clave de los pétalos
aquel ardor de alba, miel y sal.

Criatura perdida
en la maleza de la antigua mies.

Inútil es buscar lo que fue un día
lava de oro y furia de clavel.
En el nuevo nacer, frente inclinada;
sumiso, el que era antes ágil pie;
ya el pecho con escudo; ya pequeña
la custodiada sombra del laurel.

¿Quién viene ahora entre la espesa escarcha?
Duele la fría rosa de la faz
y ya no tienen los secretos ciervos,
para su dura sed, el manantial.

Angel del aire que has velado el rostro:
crece tu niebla sobre mi pleamar.

Juana de Ibarbourou
TIME

I confront you, oh life without sheaves,
from the house of my solitude.
Anchored behind me is that time
when I had passion and freedom,
my throat open to the cry of love,
and chaste nakedness, and glory.

I was a flower, oh life, and inside
I was lulled by eternity.

Shadows now, shadows on the stalk,
and no feelings now
in the cloistered key to the petals
of that ardor of dawn, honey and salt.

Lost child
in the tangle of the old fields.

Futile to seek what was one day
gold lava, and carnation's fury.
In new birth, forehead bent down;
what was once an agile foot, submissive;
now the breast with a shield; small
the sheltered shadow of the laurel.

Who comes now through the thick frost?
There is pain in the cold rose of the face
and the secret stags have no longer,
the spring for their hard thirst.

Angel of the air with veiled face:
your fog is rising over my high tide.

from *Perdida*, 1950
P.H.

Juan Ramón Jiménez   *born in Moguer, Huelva, Spain,*
December 25, 1881

died in San Juan, Puerto Rico,
May 29, 1958

The first poetry of Jiménez bears the mark of Darío's Modernism,
and later the influence of the French symbolists; but in all his work
he attempts to refine every poetic element to its most perfect state and
"to make concrete what is vague." Although this tendency leads him
to a more intellectual expression, his ability to evoke shimmering
images of light and beauty seems to grow as his work becomes more
conceptual. At 19 he published *Almas de violeta*, the first of some 32
books of poems he wrote during his lifetime. In 1905, he returned to
his birthplace, the Andalusian countryside he immortalized in poems
and in *Platero y yo*, the long prose-poem well known to American
readers. In the 1930s, Jiménez lived in Madrid's famous cultural
center, the Residencia de Estudiantes, where he met his future wife,
Zenobia Camprubí. During the civil war, Jiménez left for America,
and lived mainly in Puerto Rico. In 1956, he won the Nobel Prize for
Literature. The happiness of the achievement was shattered by his
wife's death; and he died a year and a half later.

Juan Ramón Jiménez
CUANDO, DORMIDA TU...

Cuando, dormida tú, me echo en tu alma,
y escucho, con mi oído
en tu pecho desnudo,
tu corazón tranquilo, me parece
que, en su latir hondo, sorprendo
el secreto del centro
del mundo.
      Me parece
que lejiones de ánjeles,
en caballos celestes
—como cuando, en la alta
noche escuchamos, sin aliento
y el oído en la tierra,
trotes distantes que no llegan nunca—,
que lejiones de ánjeles
vienen por tí, de lejos
—como los Reyes Magos
al nacimiento eterno
de nuestro amor—,
vienen por tí, de lejos,
a traerme, en tu ensueño,
el secreto del centro
del cielo.

Juan Ramón Jiménez
WHEN, WITH YOU ASLEEP...

When, with you asleep, I plunge into your soul,
and I listen, with my ear
on your naked breast,
to your tranquil heart, it seems to me
that, in its deep throbbing, I surprise
the secret of the center
of the world.

    It seems to me
that legions of angels
on celestial steeds
—as when, in the height
of the night we listen, without a breath
and our ears to the earth,
to distant hoofbeats that never arrive—,
that legions of angels
are coming through you, from afar
—like the Three Kings
to the eternal birth
of our love—,
they are coming through you, from afar,
to bring me, in your dreams,
the secret of the center
of the heavens.

from *Diario de un poeta recién casado*, 1917
P.H.

Juan Ramón Jiménez
VINO, PRIMERO, PURA...

Vino, primero, pura,
vestida de inocencia.
Y la amé como un niño.

Luego se fué vistiendo
de no sé qué ropajes.
Y la fuí odiando, sin saberlo.

Llegó a ser una reina,
fastuosa de tesoros...
¡Qué iracundia de yel y sin sentido!

... Mas se fué desnudando.
Y yo le sonreía.

Se quedó con la túnica
de su inocencia antigua.
Creí de nuevo en ella.

Y se quitó la túnica,
y apareció desnuda toda...
¡Oh pasión de mi vida, poesía
desnuda, mía para siempre!

Juan Ramón Jiménez
SHE CAME, AT FIRST, PURE ...

She came, at first, pure,
dressed in innocence.
And I loved her like a child.

Then she began dressing
in heaven knows what kind of clothes.
And I began hating her, without even knowing it.

She got to be a queen,
pompous with treasures.
What bitter and unfeeling rage!

... But she began undressing.
And I smiled at her.

She kept just the tunic,
of her innocence of old.
I believed in her once again.

And she took off her tunic,
and stood there completely naked ...
Oh passion of my life, poetry,
naked, mine forever!

from *Eternidades*, 1918
P.H.

Juan Ramón Jiménez
MIRLO FIEL

Cuando el mirlo, en lo verde nuevo, un día
vuelve, y silba su amor, embriagado,
meciendo su inquietud en fresco de oro,
nos abre, negro, con su rojo pico,
carbón vivificado por su ascua,
un alma de valores armoniosos
mayor que todo nuestro ser.

No cabemos, por él, redondos, plenos,
en nuestra fantasía despertada.
(El sol, mayor que el sol,
inflama el mar real o imajinario,
que resplandece entre el azul frondor,
mayor que el mar, que el mar.)
Las alturas nos vuelcan sus últimos tesoros,
preferimos la tierra donde estamos,
un momento llegamos,
en viento, en ola, en roca, en llama,
al imposible eterno de la vida.

La arquitectura eterea, delante,
con los cuatro elementos sorprendidos,
nos abre total, una,
a perspectivas inmanentes,
realidad solitaria de los sueños,
sus embelesadoras galerías.
La flor mejor se eleva a nuestra boca,
la nube es de mujer,
la fruta seno nos responde sensual.

Y el mirlo canta, huye por lo verde,
y sube, sale por lo verde, y silba,
recanta por lo verde venteante,
libre en la luz y la tersura,
torneado alegremente por el aire,
dueño completo de su placer doble;

Juan Ramón Jiménez
FAITHFUL BLACKBIRD

When the blackbird, in the new greenery, comes back
one day, and trills his love, enraptured,
rocking his restlessness in a fresco of gold,
he opens to us, in his blackness, with his red beak,
coal quickened by its ember,
a soul of harmonious values
greater than our whole being.

Because of him, we are not contained, round, full,
in our aroused fantasy.
(The sun, greater than the sun,
inflames the real or imaginary sea,
that glitters through the blue foliage,
greater than the sea, than the sea.)
The heights shower us with their ultimate treasures,
we prefer the earth where we are,
one moment we arrive,
in wind, in wave, in rock, in flame,
at the impossible eternity of life.

The ethereal architecture, ahead,
with its four elements surprised,
opens for us totally, one,
immanent perspectives,
solitary reality of dreams,
its entrancing galleries.
The finest flower rises to our mouths
the cloud is woman,
the fruit breast responds to us, sensual.

And the blackbird sings, wings away through the greenery,
and rises, climbs above the greenery, and sings,
he retreats through the breezy greenery,
free in the light and glossiness,
happily tossed by the wind,
complete master of his double pleasure;

entra, vibra silbando, ríe, habla,
canta... Y ensancha con su canto
la hora parada de la estación viva,
y nos hace la vida suficiente.

¡Eternidad, hora ensanchada,
paraíso de lustror único, abierto
a nosotros mayores, pensativos,
por un ser diminuto que se ensancha!
¡Primavera, absoluta primavera,
cuando el mirlo ejemplar, una mañana,
enloquece de amor entre lo verde!

he enters, quivers as he whistles, laughs, speaks,
sings . . . And he lengthens with his song
the suspended hour of the living season,
and makes our life sufficient.

Eternity, broadened moment,
paradise of unique splendor opened
to us, who are larger, thinking creatures,
by a diminutive puffed up being!
Spring, absolute Spring,
when the exemplary blackbird, one morning,
goes crazy with love in the greenery!

from *La estación total*, 1946
P.H.

Sor Juana Inés de la Cruz

born Juana de Asbaje in San Miguel de Nepantla (or Amecameca), Mexico, November 12, 1651

died in Mexico City, Mexico, April 17, 1691 or 1695

Sor Juana Inés de la Cruz was a tireless defender of learning and scholarship. She was inspired by the Spanish masters of the Golden Age, Góngora and Quevedo, whose elaborate images and intricate conceptual use of language decorate a basically pessimistic view of life. She was called Mexico's "Décima musa" (10th Muse) and she is still celebrated today for her passionate poetry and as the greatest Spanish American lyric poet of the colonial period. Her father was a Basque and her mother a creole; apparently they never married. As a young girl she became an accomplished musician and performed scientific experiments. Women at that time were not allowed to attend the university, and so the impressive erudition she attained was all the more remarkable. She entered a convent when she was 16, some say because of the death of her lover, whom she was to marry. At 17 she astounded a board of some forty professors with her knowledge. And although religious authorities reprimanded her for her classical scholarship and scientific curiosity, Sor Juana was able to put together the finest library in Mexico at that time. She died in her early forties, after nursing plague victims in the streets of Mexico City.

Sor Juana Inés de la Cruz
DETENTE, SOMBRA DE
MI BIEN ESQUIVO...

Detente, sombra de mi bien esquivo,
imagen del hechizo que más quiero,
bella ilusión por quien alegre muero,
dulce ficción por quien penosa vivo.

Si al imán de tus gracias, atractivo,
sirve mi pecho de obediente acero,
¿para qué me enamoras lisonjero
si has de burlarme luego fugitivo?

Mas blasonar no puedes, satisfecho,
de que triunfa de mí tu tiranía:
que aunque dejas burlado el lazo estrecho

que tu forma fantástica ceñía,
poco importa burlar brazos y pecho
si te labra prisión mi fantasía.

Sor Juana Inés de la Cruz
STOP, SHADOW OF
MY ELUSIVE BELOVED

Stop, shadow of my elusive beloved,
image of enchantment that I most desire,
beautiful illusion for whom I happily die,
sweet fiction for whom I painfully live.

If to the magnet of your graces, attractive,
my breast serves as obedient steel,
why do you capture my love in such pleasure
if you are to leave me later, fugitive?

But you cannot boast, satisfied,
that your tyranny triumphs over me:
for though you have eluded the tight noose

that encircled your fantastic form,
it matters little to deceive arms and breast
if I fashion a prison for you in my fantasy.

About 1690
from *Obras completas*, 1957
P.H.

Lope de Vega

born in Puerta de Guadalajara, Madrid, Spain, November 25, 1562

died in Madrid, August 27, 1635

Lope de Vega's poems are characterized by a feeling of love for humanity. He wrote in folkloric, religious, comic and baroque styles; and most of his poems were written in dramatic form, intended to be understood in the popular theater. Born to a humble family, he wrote the first of his 1800 plays at 13. After four years at the University of Alcalá, he became the personal secretary of the Duke of Alba. It was then that he fell in love with Elena Osorio, the first of many amorous liaisons. At 26 he served as a crewman on one of the ships in Spain's "Invincible Armada." By this time he was a celebrated playwright. He married Isabel de Urbina whom he immortalized in poems and plays as Belisa. After her death, he married at least three other times. In 1614 he took religious orders, and was important in the Church despite his continual love affairs.

Lope de Vega
ES LA MUJER DEL HOMBRE
LO MÁS BUENO...

Es la mujer del hombre lo más bueno,
y locura decir que lo más malo;
su vida suele ser y su regalo,
su muerte suele ser y su veneno.

Cielo a los ojos cándido y sereno,
que muchas veces al infierno igualo;
por raro al mundo su valor señalo;
por falso al hombre su rigor condeno.

Ella nos da su sangre, ella nos cría;
no ha hecho el cielo cosa más ingrata;
es un ángel y a veces una harpía;

quiere, aborrece, trata bien, maltrata,
y es la mujer, al fin, como sangría,
que a veces da salud y a veces mata.

Lope de Vega
WOMAN IS OF MAN
THE BEST...

Woman is of man the best,
and insane it is to say the worst;
his life she is and his great gift,
his poison is she and his death.

Heaven to the eyes chaste and serene,
Which often to hell I compare,
for her courage, I tell the world she is rare,
for false to man her rigor I condemn.

She gives us her blood, she rears us all:
Heaven has not made a more ungrateful thing;
she is an angel, and sometimes she's the devil.

She loves, abhors, treats well, treats ill,
and it's woman, after all, like a bleeding,
that sometimes cures, and sometimes kills.

About 1602
from *Poesía lírica de Lope de Vega*, 1964
P.H.

Ramón López Velarde   *born in Ciudad García, Zacatecas, México, June 15, 1888*

died in Mexico City, June 19, 1921

Ramón López Velarde's best known work is "La Suave Patria" (1932), a long patriotic poem written in the Modernist style, but expressing the hope of post-revolutionary Mexico and introducing the varied language and customs of the rural people who give the country its identity. His other poems are more personal in nature and deal with small and intimate moments. As a student, López Verlarde wrote his first poems at the Conciliar Seminary in Aguascalientes. Friends report that he wrote poems with some words left out and would supply appropriate words spontaneously as he read them aloud. He earned a law degree, served as a judge, then moved to Mexico City in 1914 during the Revolution. He held a post in the Department of the Interior and taught after 1916.

Ramón López Velarde
MI PRIMA AGUEDA

Mi madrina invitaba a mi prima Agueda
a que pasara el día con nosotros,
y mi prima llegaba
con un contradictorio
prestigio de almidón y de temible
luto ceremonioso.

Agueda aparecía, resonante
de almidón, y sus ojos
verdes y sus mejillas rubicundas
me protegían contra el pavoroso
luto . . .
      Yo era rapaz
y conocía la "o" por lo redondo,
y Agueda que tejía
mansa y perseverante en el sonoro
corredor, me causaba
calosfríos ignotos . . .
(Creo que hasta la debo la costumbre
heroicamente insana de hablar solo.)

A la hora de comer, en la penumbra
quieta del refectorio,
me iba embelesando un quebradizo
sonar intermitente de vajilla
y el timbre caricioso
de la voz de mi prima.
            Agueda era
(luto, pupilas verdes y mejillas
rubicundas) un cesto policromo
de manzanas y uvas
en el ébano de un armario añoso.

Ramón López Velarde
MY COUSIN AGATHA

My godmother invited my cousin Agatha
to spend the day with us,
and my cousin arrived
with a contradictory
prestige of starch and of fearful
ceremonious mourning.

Agatha appeared, resonant
in starch, and her eyes
of green and her rosy cheeks
protected me from the frightful
mourning . . .

    I was a lad
and I knew an "o" by its roundness,
and Agatha who knitted
gentle and perservering in the sonorous
hall, gave me
unknown chills . . .
(I think that I even owe her the habit,
heroically insane, of talking alone)

At supper time, in the quiet
twilight of the dining room,
I was slowly entranced by a delicate
intermittent sound of dishes
and the caressing timbre
of my cousin's voice.
                    Agatha was
(mourning, green eyes and rosy cheeks)
a polychromatic basket
of apples and grapes
on the ebony of an age-old wardrobe.

from *La sangre devota*, 1916
P.H.

Federico García Lorca

*born in Fuentevaqueros, Granada,
Spain, June 11, 1898*

*died near Viznar, Granada,
August 19, 1936*

Virtually all of Federico García Lorca's works have a strong flavor of
the folklore and mysteries of the old cultures of Southern Spain,
particularly the gypsies (*Romancero gitano*, 1927). In his many
poems about love, the dreamlike surreal images frequently express an
underlying sense of violence and an awareness of death. He loved
music (Manuel de Falla was one of his idols) and art, and became a
fine pianist and artist as well as a renowned poet and dramatist. In
1929, he studied at Columbia University (*Poeta en Nueva York*,
1929-30, is a poetic vision of his experience there), traveled in Canada
and Cuba, and in 1933-34 toured Uruguay and Argentina with a
theater group. In 1936 Lorca returned to Madrid, where he wrote and
directed plays under the Republic. In Granada, on a visit to his
family, Franco's Falangist squad arrested him, and he was shot
somewhere in the mountains the following day. No one knows
exactly where his body lies. His death became a rallying point for
intellectuals and artists worldwide who opposed the Franco regime.

Federico García Lorca
SERENATA

(Homenaje a Lope de Vega)

Por las orillas del río
se está la noche mojando
y en los pechos de Lolita
se mueren de amor los ramos.

Se mueren de amor los ramos.

La noche canta desnuda
sobre los puentes de marzo.
Lolita lava su cuerpo
con agua salobre y nardos.

Se mueren de amor los ramos.

La noche de anís y plata
relumbra por los tejados.
Plata de arroyos y espejos.
Anís de tus muslos blancos.

Se mueren de amor los ramos.

Federico García Lorca
SERENADE

(Homage to Lope de Vega)

Along the banks of the river
the night is getting wet
and on the breasts of Lolita
the branches are dying of love.

The branches are dying of love.

The night is singing naked
over the bridges of March.
Lolita is washing her body
with brackish water and nards.

The branches are dying of love.

The night of anise and silver
glares on the rooftops.
Silver of streams and mirrors.
Anise of your white thighs.

The branches are dying of love.

from *Canciones*; *1921-1924,* 1927
P.H.

Federico García Lorca
GACELA DEL AMOR IMPREVISTO

Nadie comprendía el perfume
de la oscura magnolia de tu vientre.
Nadie sabía que martirizabas
un colibrí de amor entre los dientes.

Mil caballitos persas se dormían
en la plaza con luna de tu frente,
mientras que yo enlazaba cuatro noches
tu cintura, enemiga de la nieve.

Entre yeso y jazmines, tu mirada
era un pálido ramo de simientes.
Yo busqué, para darte, por mi pecho
las letras de marfil que dicen siempre,

siempre, siempre: jardín de mi agonía,
tu cuerpo fugitivo para siempre,
la sangre de tus venas en mi boca,
tu boca ya sin luz para mi muerte.

Federico García Lorca
GHAZEL OF UNFORSEEN LOVE

No one could perceive the perfume
of the dark magnolia of your womb.
No one knew that you martyrized
a hummingbird of love between your teeth.

A thousand persian ponies were falling asleep
in the plaza with the moonlight from your forehead,
while I held fast for four nights
around your waist, enemy of snows.

Between chalk and jasmines, your look
was a pale branch of seed.
I searched, to give you, through my breast
the letters of ivory that say always,

always, always: garden of my agony,
your body fleeing forever,
the blood of your veins in my mouth,
your mouth now without light for my death.

from *Diván del Tamarit*, 1936
P.H.

Antonio Machado

born in Seville, Spain, July, 1875

died in Collioure, France,
February 22, 1939

Antonio Machado is one of Spain's greatest 20th-century poets. His poems are monumental and somber, and as Ruben Darío said, evoke "mystery and silence" of the stark Castillian landscape where he spent much of his life. As he grew up in Madrid, he associated with literary figures and theater people. At 24, he attended the College of France in Paris where he met Oscar Wilde and Jean Moréas. In 1902, he met Rubén Darío whose influence is present in his earliest poems. He taught French in Soria, where he married Leonor Izquierdo. She was 16 and he 35; it was a happy marriage but she died only three years later. During the civil war, Machado supported the Republic. When defeat became inevitable, Machado and his mother, both of them in poor health, fled to France on foot. He died in Collioure a month later.

Antonio Machado
EL TREN

Yo, para todo viaje
—siempre sobre la madera
de mi vagón de tercera—,
voy ligero de equipaje.
Si es de noche, porque no
acostumbro a dormir yo,
y de día, por mirar
los arbolitos pasar,
yo nunca duermo en el tren,
y, sin embargo, voy bien.
¡Este placer de alejarse!
Londres, Madrid, Ponferrada,
tan lindos . . . para marcharse.
Lo molesto es la llegada.
Luego, el tren, el caminar,
siempre nos hace soñar;
y casi, casi olvidamos
el jamelgo que montamos.
¡Oh, el pollino
que sabe bien el camino!
¿Dónde estamos?
¿Dónde todos nos bajamos?
¡Frente a mí va una monjita
tan bonita!
Tiene esa expresión serena
que a la pena
da una esperanza infinita.
Y yo pienso: Tú eres buena;
porque diste tus amores
a Jesús; porque no quieres
ser madre de pecadores.
Mas tú eres
maternal,
bendita entre las mujeres,
madrecita virginal.

Antonio Machado
THE TRAIN

Every time I take a trip
—always on the wooden seat
of my third-class car—
I travel light.
If it's at night, because I'm
not used to sleeping,
and if it's day, so I can see
the little trees going by,
I never sleep on the train,
but, nonetheless, I don't mind.
What a pleasure to get away!
London, Madrid, Ponferrada,
pretty places . . . just to go and see.
The trouble is you get there.
Besides, the traveling, the train,
always makes us dream;
and we almost, almost forget
the tired old horse we are riding.
Oh, the pony
that knows the trail well!
Where are we?
Where do we all bid farewell?
A little nun is sitting before me
she is very pretty!
She has that serene look
which to grief
gives a feeling of infinite hope.
And I think: You are so good;
because you gave your love
to Jesus; so as not to become
a mother of sinners.
But you are
maternal
blessed among women,
sweetly motherly maiden.

Algo en tu rostro es divino
bajo tus cofias de lino.
Tus mejillas
—esas rosas amarillas—
fueron rosadas, y, luego,
ardió en tus entrañas fuego;
y hoy, esposa de la Cruz,
ya eres luz, y sólo luz...
¡Todas las mujeres bellas
fueran, como tú, doncellas
en un convento a encerrarse!...
¡Y la niña que yo quiero,
ay, preferirá casarse
con un mocito barbero!
El tren camina y camina,
y la máquina resuella,
y tose con tos ferina.
¡Vamos en una centella!

Something in your face is divine
beneath your flaxen locks.
Your cheeks
—those yellow roses—
were rosy once, and, then,
burned a fire deep within;
and today, wife of the Cross,
now you are light, and only light . . .
I wish all beautiful women
would go, like you, still maiden,
to a convent and hide themselves away! . . .
And the girl that I love
ah, will probably want to marry
some silly young barber.
The train keeps on rolling on
and the locomotive puffs
and coughs a hacking cough.
We're gone in a flash!

from *Campos de Castilla*, 1912
P.H.

Antonio Machado
EL AMOR Y LA SIERRA

Cabalgaba por agria serranía,
una tarde, entre roca cenicienta.
El plomizo balón de la tormenta
de monte en monte rebotar se oía.

Súbito, al vivo resplandor del rayo,
se encabritó, bajo de un alto pino,
al borde de una peña, su caballo.
A dura rienda le tornó al camino.

Y hubo visto la nube desgarrada,
y, dentro, la afilada crestería
de otra sierra más lueñe y levantada

—relámpago de piedra parecía—.
¿Y vio el rostro de Dios? Vio el de su amada.
Gritó: ¡Morir en esta sierra fría!

Antonio Machado

LOVE AND THE MOUNTAINS

He rode through bitter mountains,
one evening, among ashen rocks.
The leaden ball of the storm
from peak to peak he heard rebound.

Suddenly, in the quickness of the lightning's light,
beneath a tall pine, his horse,
at the brink of a cliff, reared and shied.
A heavy rein turned him back to his course.

And he had seen the cloud torn open,
and the jagged crest inside
of another range, far off and high above

—lightning of stone it brought to mind—.
And did he see the face of God? He saw his love's.
He cried: Oh in these cold hills to die!

from *Nuevas canciones*, 1925
P.H.

Gabriela Mistral

*born in Lucila Godoy Alcayaga,
Vicuña, in the Elqui Valley, Chile,
April 7, 1889*

*died in Hempstead, Long Island, New
York, January 10, 1957*

The American landscape and its people are present in Gabriela
Mistral's poetry. Nearly all of her poems express some aspect of love,
including love for fellow human beings, the love of nature, and
religious love. Gabriela Mistral was raised by her mother in Monte
Grande, a small town in Northern Chile. She was a timid child, yet
in spite of an irregular early education, the gifted young poet was
teaching in rural Chilean schools by 1904. At 18, she fell in love with
a railroad worker and, although they broke up after only a year, she
was deeply affected by his suicide a few years later. Her fame grew
outside Chile until, in the early 1920s, the Mexican Minister of
Education invited her to help revise the Mexican school system. This
was the first of many diplomatic assignments that took her all over
the world. Although she never married, she adopted a nephew,
Gingin (Yinyin). Tragically, he took his own life at the age of 15.
This news reached Mistral just before she received the Nobel Prize for
Literature in the Fall of 1945. She spent the last years of her life in
the United States where she taught in several New England
universities.

Gabriela Mistral
EL VASO

Yo sueño con un vaso de humilde y simple arcilla,
que guarde tus cenizas cerca de mis miradas;
y la pared del vaso te será mi mejilla,
y quedarán mi alma y tu alma apaciguadas.

No quiero espolvorearlas en vaso de oro ardiente,
ni en la ánfora pagana que carnal línea ensaya:
sólo un vaso de arcilla te ciña simplemente,
humildemente, como un pliegue de mi saya.

En una tarde de éstas recogeré la arcilla
por el río, y lo haré con pulso tembloroso.
Pasarán las mujeres cargadas de gavillas,
y no sabrán que amaso el lecho de un esposo.

El puñado de polvo, que cabe entre mis manos,
se verterá sin ruido, como una hebra de llanto.
Yo sellaré este vaso con beso sobrehumano,
¡y mi mirada inmensa será tu único manto!

Gabriela Mistral
THE VASE

I dream of a vase of humble and simple clay,
to keep your ashes near my watchful eyes;
and for you my cheek will be the wall of the vase
and my soul and your soul will be satisfied.

I will not sift them into a vase of burning gold,
nor into a pagan urn that mimics carnal lines:
I want only a vase of simple clay to hold
you humbly like a fold in this skirt of mine.

One of these afternoons I'll gather the clay
by the river, and I'll shape it with trembling hand.
Women, bearing sheaves, will pass my way,
not guessing I fashion a bed for a husband.

The fistful of dust, I hold in my hands,
will noiselessly pour, like a thread of tears.
I will seal this vase with an infinite kiss,
and I'll cover you only with my endless gaze!

from *Desolación*, 1922
P.H.

Gabriela Mistral
EL AMOR QUE CALLA

Si yo te odiara, mi odio te daría
en las palabras, rotundo y seguro;
pero te amo y mi amor no se confía
a este hablar de los hombres, tan oscuro.

Tú lo quisieras vuelto un alarido,
y viene de tan hondo que ha deshecho
su quemante raudal, desfallecido,
antes de la garganta, antes del pecho.

Estoy lo mismo que estanque colmado
y te parezco un surtidor inerte.
¡Todo por mi callar atribulado
que es más atroz que el entrar en la muerte!

Gabriela Mistral
SILENT LOVE

If I hated you, I would give you my hate
in words, full and sure;
but I love you, and my love does not put faith
in mere words of men, so obscure.

You would like it changed to an outcry,
yet its burning torrent of flame comes from such depth
that it has fallen apart, died,
before reaching to my throat, before my breast.

I feel just like a brimming pool,
and to you I seem a lifeless fount.
All because of my painful silence
more atrocious than facing death itself.

from *Desolación*, 1922
P.H.

Gabriela Mistral
MECIENDO

El mar sus millares de olas
    mece, divino.
Oyendo a los mares amantes,
    mezo a mi niño.

El viento errabundo en la noche
    mece los trigos.
Oyendo a los vientos amantes,
    mezo a mi niño.

Dios padre sus miles de mundos
    mece sin ruido.
Sintiendo su mano en la sombra
    mezo a mi niño.

Gabriela Mistral
ROCKING MY CHILD

The sea its millions of waves
    is rocking, divine,
hearing the loving seas,
    I'm rocking my child.

The wandering wind in the night
    is rocking the fields of wheat,
hearing the loving winds,
    I'm rocking my child.

God the father his thousands of worlds
    is rocking without a sound.
Feeling his hand in the shadows,
    I'm rocking my child.

from *Ternura*, 1925
P.H.

Pablo Neruda

born Ricardo Neftalí Reyes, in Parral, Chile, July 12, 1904

died in Santiago, Chile, September 23, 1973

Pablo Neruda's most popular early poems are in the surreal *Residencias* (1933, 1935, 1947), but he is best known for his politically and socially "compromised" poetry in *Canto General* (1950). Neruda's poems express a common bond of love, respect, and desire for freedom among the people of the Americas (this is more his "communism" than is his political affiliation). His many beautiful love poems contain sincere and intimate images. Pablo Neruda never knew his real mother who died scarcely a month after he was born; his father worked for the railroad. One of young Neruda's teachers in the Temuco schools was Nobel Prize-winning poet Gabriela Mistral. As a boy he loved to write poetry, but had to conceal it from his family, who thought it an unmanly activity and a waste of time. After a period of financial difficulty, he obtained a government post in Burma, where he wrote many of the poems in *Residencia en la tierra* (1933). He served as a diplomat in many different countries: Ceylon, Java, Singapore, Argentina, Spain, and later in Mexico. From the time Neruda joined the Communist Party in Chile in 1945, to his support of Salvador Allende, he had an active political career. He received the Nobel Prize for Literature in 1971, and died only 12 days after the Pinochet coup in 1973.

Pablo Neruda
JUVENTUD

Un perfume como una ácida espada
de ciruelas en un camino,
los besos del azúcar en los dientes,
las gotas vitales resbalando en los dedos,
la dulce pulpa erótica,
las eras, los pajares, los incitantes
sitios secretos de las casas anchas,
los colchones dormidos en el pasado, el agrio valle verde
mirado desde arriba, desde el vidrio escondido:
toda la adolescencia mojándose y ardiendo
como una lámpara derribada en la lluvia.

Pablo Neruda
YOUTH

A perfume like an acid sword
of plums on a road,
the kisses of sugar on your teeth,
the vital drops sliding on your fingers,
the sweet erotic pulp,
the gardens, the haylofts, the inciting
secret places in the huge houses,
the mattresses asleep in the past, the bitter green valley
seen from above, from the hidden glass:
all adolescence getting wet and burning
like an oil lamp dropped in the rain.

from *Canto general*, 1950
P.H.

Pablo Neruda

LA LLUVIA (RAPA NUI)

No, que la Reina no reconozca
tu rostro, es más dulce
así, amor mío, lejos de las efigies, el peso
de tu cabellera en mis manos, recuerdas
el árbol de Mangarevea cuyas flores caían
sobre tu pelo? Estos dedos no se parecen
a los pétalos blancos: míralos, son como raíces,
son como tallos de piedra sobre los que resbala
el lagarto. No temas, esperemos que caiga la lluvia, desnudos,
la lluvia, la misma que cae sobre Manu Tara.

Pero así como el agua endurece sus rasgos en la piedra,
sobre nosotros cae llevándonos suavemente
hacia la oscuridad, más abajo del agujero de Ranu Raraku.
                                           Por eso
que no te divise el pescador ni el cántaro, Sepulta
tus pechos de quemadura gemela en mi boca,
y que tu cabellera sea una pequeña noche mía,
una oscuridad cuyo perfume mojado me cubre.

De noche sueño que tú y yo somos dos plantas
que se elevaron juntas, con raíces enredadas,
y que tú conoces la tierra y la lluvia como mi boca,
porque de tierra y de lluvia estamos hechos. A veces

pienso que con la muerte dormiremos abajo,
en la profundidad de los pies de la efigie, mirando
el Océano que nos trajo a construir y a amar.

Mis manos no eran férreas cuando te conocieron, las aguas
de otro mar las pasaban como a una red; ahora
agua y piedras sostienen semillas y secretos.

Pablo Neruda
THE RAIN (RAPA NUI)

No, the Queen must not look upon
your face, it is much sweeter
this way, my love, far from the effigies, the weight
of your long tresses in my hands, do you remember
the tree in Mangareva whose flowers fell
on your hair? These fingers do not resemble
its petals of white: look at them, they are like roots,
they are like stems of stone where we see the lizard
glide. Do not be afraid, let us wait for the rain to fall, naked,
the rain, the same rain that is falling over Manu Tara.

But just as the water hardens its features on stone,
it falls upon us carrying us gently
into darkness, beneath the hollow of Ranu Raraku.
                             So that
neither the fisherman nor the crater shall notice. Bury
your breasts of twin flame in my mouth,
and let your long hair be my own small night,
a darkness covering me with its moist perfume.

    By night I dream that you and I are two plants
    that grew together, with roots entangled,
    and that you know the earth and the rain like my mouth,
    for of earth and rain are we made. Sometimes
    I think that we will sleep with death below,
    down at the effigies' feet, watching
    the Ocean that brought us to build and to love.

My hands were not like iron when they first knew you,
                           the waters
of another sea slipped through them as through a net; now
water and stones sustain seeds and secrets.

Ámame dormida y desnuda, que en la orilla
eres como la isla: tu amor confuso, tu amor
asombrado, escondido en la cavidad de los sueños,
es como el movimiento del mar que nos rodea.

Y cuando yo también vaya durmiéndome
en tu amor, desnudo,
deja mi mano entre tus pechos para que palpite
al mismo tiempo que tus pezones mojados en la lluvia.

Love me sleeping and naked, for on the shore
you are like the island: your perplexed love, your love
astonished, hidden in the hollow of dreams,
is like the moving sea around us.

And when I too start drifting off to sleep
in your love, naked,
let my hand remain between your breasts so it may tremble
with your wet nipples in the rain.

from *Canto general*, 1950
C.J.

Pablo Neruda
ODA A SU AROMA

Suave mía, a qué hueles,
a qué fruto,
a qué estrella, a qué hoja?

Cerca
de tu pequeña oreja
o en tu frente
me inclino,
clavo
la nariz entre el pelo
y la sonrisa
buscando, conociendo
la raza de tu aroma:
es suave, pero
no es flor, no es cuchillada
de clavel penetrante
o arrebatado aroma
de violentos
jazmines,
es algo, es tierra,
es
aire,
maderas o manzanas,
olor
de la luz en la piel,
aroma
de la hoja
del árbol
de la vida
con polvo
de camino
y frescura
de matutina sombra
en las raíces,
olor de piedra y río,
pero

Pablo Neruda
ODE TO HER AROMA

My soft woman, what do you smell of,
of what fruits
of what star, of what leaf?

Near
your small ear
or upon your forehead
I lean over,
I thrust
my nose in your hair
and your smile
seeking, knowing
the breed of your aroma:
it is soft, but
not a flower, not the slash
of penetrating carnation
or the reckless aroma
of violent
jasmines,
it is something, it is earth
it is
air,
wood or apples,
the odor
of light on skin,
aroma
of the leaf
of the tree
of life
with dust
of the road
and freshness
of early morning shadow
in the roots,
odor of stone and river,
but

161

más cerca
de un durazno,
de la tibia
palpitación secreta
de la sangre,
olor
a casa pura
y a cascada,
fragancia
de paloma
y caballera,
aroma
de mi mano
que recorrió la luna
de tu cuerpo,
las estrellas
de tu piel estrellada,
el oro,
el trigo,
el pan de tu contacto,
y allí
en la longitud
de tu luz loca,
en tu circunferencia de vasija,
en la copa,
en los ojos de tus senos, ·
entre tus anchos párpados
y tu boca de espuma,
en todo
dejó,
dejó mi mano
olor de tinta y selva,
sangre y frutos perdidos,
fragancia
de olvidados planetas,
de puros
papeles vegetales,
allí
mi propio cuerpo
sumergido

closer
to a peach
to the warm
secret palpitation
of blood,
odor
of a pure house
and of a waterfall,
fragrance
of a dove
and hair,
aroma
of my hand
that crisscrossed the moon
of your body,
the stars
of your starry skin,
the gold,
the wheat,
the bread of your contact,
and there
in the longitude
of your crazy light,
on your vaselike circumference,
in the cup,
on the eyes of your breasts,
between your wide eyelids,
and your mouth of foam,
on everything
it left,
my hand left
the odor of ink and forest,
blood and lost fruit,
fragrance
of forgotten planets,
of pure
vegetable papers,
there
my own body
submerged

en la frescura de tu amor, amada,
como en un manantial
o en el sonido
de un campanario
arriba
entre el olor del cielo
y el vuelo
de las últimas aves,
amor,
olor,
palabra
de tu piel, del idioma
de la noche en tu noche,
del día en tu mirada.

Desde tu corazón
sube
tu aroma
como desde la tierra
la luz hasta la cima del cerezo:
en tu piel yo detengo
tu latido
y huelo
la ola de luz que sube,
la fruta sumergida
en su fragancia,
la noche que respiras,
la sangre que recorre
tu hermosura
hasta llegar al beso
que me espera
en tu boca.

in the freshness of your love, my love,
as in a spring
or in the sound
of a belfry
above
between the odor of the sky
and the flight
of the last birds of day
love,
odor,
word
of your skin, from the language
of the night in your night,
of the day in your eyes.

From your heart
rises
your aroma
as from the earth
light rises to the top of the cherry tree:
on your skin I detain
your pulse
and I smell
the wave of light that rises,
the fruit submerged
in its fragrance,
the night that you breathe,
the blood that runs through
your beauty
until it arrives in the kiss
that awaits me
in your mouth.

from *Nuevas odas elementales*, 1956
P.H.

Pablo Neruda
PLENA MUJER, MANZANA CARNAL...

Plena mujer, manzana carnal, luna caliente,
espeso aroma de algas, lodo y luz machacados,
qué oscura claridad se abre entre tus columnas?
Qué antigua noche el hombre toca con sus sentidos?

Ay, amar es un viaje con agua y con estrellas,
con aire ahogado y bruscas tempestades de harina:
amar es un combate de relámpagos
y dos cuerpos por una sola miel derrotados.

Beso a beso recorro tu pequeño infinito,
tus márgenes, tus ríos, tus pueblos diminutos,
y el fuego genital transformado en delicia

corre por los delgados caminos de la sangre
hasta precipitarse como un clavel nocturno,
hasta ser y no ser sino un rayo en la sombra.

Pablo Neruda
FULL WOMAN, CARNAL APPLE...

Full woman, carnal apple, hot moon,
dense aroma of crushed seaweed, mud and light,
what obscure clarity opens between your columns?
What ancient night does man touch with his senses?

Oh, loving is a journey with water and stars,
with stifled air and brusque tempests of flour:
loving is a combat of lightning bolts
and two bodies defeated by a single drop of honey.

Kiss by kiss I traverse your small infinity,
your edges, your rivers, your tiny villages,
and the genital fire transformed into delicacy

runs along the slender paths of blood
until plunging headlong like a carnation of the night,
until it is and is no more than lightning in the darkness.

XII, from *Cien sonetos de amor*, 1959
P.H.

Pablo Neruda
LA GRAN LLUVIA DEL SUR...

La gran lluvia del Sur cae sobre Isla Negra
como una sola gota transparente y pesada,
el mar abre sus hojas frías y la recibe,
la tierra aprende el húmedo destino de una copa.

Alma mía, dame en tu beso el agua
salobre de estos meses, la miel del territorio,
la fragancia mojada por mil labios del cielo,
la paciencia sagrada del mar en el invierno.

Algo nos llama, todas las puertas se abren solas,
relata el agua un largo rumor a las ventanas,
crece el cielo hacia abajo tocando las raíces,

y así teje y desteje su red celeste el día
con tiempo, sal, susurros, crecimientos, caminos,
una mujer, un hombre, y el invierno en la tierra.

Pablo Neruda
THE GREAT RAIN OF THE SOUTH...

The great rain of the South is falling on Isla Negra
like one heavy and transparent drop,
the sea opens its cold leaves and receives it,
the earth learns the wet destiny of a cup.

My love, give me in your kiss the briny water
of these months, the honey of the territory,
the fragrance moistened by a thousand lips of the sky,
the sacred patience of the sea in Winter.

Something calls us, all the doors open by themselves,
the water relates a long rumor to the windows,
the sky grows downward touching the roots,

and so the day weaves and unravels its celestial net
with time, salt, whispers, tides, roadways,
a woman, a man, and Winter on the earth.

LXVII, from *Cien sonetos de amor*, 1959
P.H

Pablo Neruda
EL HIJO

Ay hijo, sabes, sabes
de dónde vienes?

De un lago con gaviotas
blancas y hambrientas.

Junto al agua de invierno
ella y yo levantamos
una fogata roja
gastándonos los labios
de besarnos el alma,
echando al fuego todo,
quemándonos la vida.

Así llegaste al mundo.

Pero ella para verme
y para verte un día
atravesó los mares
y yo para abrazar
su pequeña cintura
toda la tierra anduve,
con guerras y montañas,
con arenas y espinas.

Así llegaste al mundo.

De tantos sitios vienes,
del agua y de la tierra,
del fuego y de la nieve,
de tan lejos caminas
hacia nosotros dos,
desde el amor terrible
que nos ha encadenado,
que queremos saber

Pablo Neruda
OUR CHILD

Oh child, do you know, do you know
where you come from?

From a lake
with white and hungry sea gulls.

Besides the wintry water
she and I built
a red bonfire
wearing away our lips
from kissing each other's souls,
throwing everything into the fire,
burning up our life.

This is the way you arrived in the world.

But in order to see me
and in order to see you one day
she crossed over the seas
and in order to embrace
her small waist
I walked the whole earth,
with wars and mountains,
with sand and spines.

This is the way you arrived in the world.

From so many places you come,
from the water and from the earth,
from the fire and from the snow,
from so far away you walk
toward the two of us,
from the terrible love
that has enchained us,
so we want to know

cómo eres, qué nos dices,
porque tú sabes más
del mundo que te dimos.

Como una gran tormenta
sacudimos nosotros
el árbol de la vida
hasta las más ocultas
fibras de las raíces
y apareces ahora
cantando en el follaje,
en la más alta rama
que contigo alcanzamos.

what you are like, what you say to us,
because you know more
about the world than we gave you.

Like a great storm
the two of us shake
the tree of life
down to the most hidden
fibers of its roots
and you appear now,
singing in the leaves,
on the highest branch
we reached with you.

from *Los versos del capitán*, 1952
P.H.

Luis Palés Matos

born in Guayama, Puerto Rico,
March 20, 1898

died in Santurce, Puerto Rico,
February 23, 1959

Luis Palés Matos is best known for his Afro-Antillean poems. Some of them are nearly pure musical and rhythmic compositions, and others present graphic, often ironic, images of black Puerto Rican society. But he also produced highly imaginative work inspired by aspects of Modernism and the Spanish Baroque, characterized by a dreamlike, fantastic atmosphere. One of his first jobs was as assistant editor of a Guayama literary magazine, *Pancho Ibero*. At 18, he married; the couple named their son Edgardo, after Edgar Allan Poe. Following his wife's death, Palés Matos moved to San Juan where he worked as a newspaperman. He loved the capital's opera and theater, acted in plays, and was known for his fine singing voice. In 1950, he lectured in the United States on tour, the only time he left Puerto Rico. During the 1950s, as his reputation grew, he became Poet-in-Residence at the University of Puerto Rico.

Luis Palés Matos
EL PECADO VIRTUOSO

Delgada y fina, te ilumina una
claridad tenue y lírica de luna,
que cae sobre tu cuerpo, plateando
la pierna fácil, el abdomen blando,
y la espalda que es huerto suave y breve
donde el rocío se ha perlado en nieve.

Delgada y fina, así, toda plateada,
la amada es una verdadera amada.
El beso es flor, el tálmo de amores
campo, y por eso está lleno de flores.
La palabra es un pájaro que trina;
la luz se da a alumbrar con fiel recato,
y en la vaga penumbra cristalina
somos, para el pecado, gata y gato . . .
pero no, que la alcoba perfumada,
sueña con el amado y con la amada,
y sí son esta amada y este amado
un cuento de hada donde no hay pecado;
pero no, porque tiene el dulce arrimo
azúcar de candor y miel de mimo,
aunque discurra por el tibio apego
una corriente erótica de fuego.
Y así, llegue la noche y nos envuelva,
como a dos niños solos en la selva.

¿Y dónde está el camino? ¿Y la casita
blanca de la pequeña viejecita?
¿Y la aldea cristiana y la campana
cristiana que repica en la mañana?
Nada se vé, mi amor, hemos salido
y en este extraño bosque hemos caído;
pero yo soy el niño que defiende
a la niña del Sátiro y del Duende.

Luis Palés Matos
THE VIRTUOUS SIN

" 'Tis the forest primeval"
—Longfellow

Slender and fine, a lyric and tenuous
moonlight illumines you,
falls upon your body, silvering
your soft abdomen, your leg, yielding,
and your back which is a brief and tender garden
where the dew has pearled into snow.

Slender and fine, all silvered,
my beloved is a true beloved.
The kiss is a flower, the wedding bed of lovers
a field, and so is filled with flowers.
A word is a trilling bird;
the light illuminates with faithful reserve,
and in the vague crystalline penumbra
we are, just two cats, as far as sin is concerned...
but no, the bedroom sweet with perfume,
dreams about two lovers, a man and a woman,
and truly, these two lovers, this woman and man,
are a fairy tale where there is no sin,
but no, because the sweet longing
holds sugar of candor and honey of caring,
though running through the warm desire
is an erotic current of fire.
And so, may the night arrive and surround us,
like it would two children alone in the forest.

And where is the pathway?
And the little white house of the little old lady?
And the Christian village and the Christian bell
which peals in the morning?
Nothing is there, my love, we have left,
and in this strange wood we fell;
but I am the boy who protects
the little girl from the Satyr and the Elf.

No te apures, mi amor, que ya crepita
la hoguera para el lobo y para el frío.
Echa tu corazón de margarita
que ya en los leños se consume el mío;
y durante la noche estará ardiendo,
tu miedo y tu belleza defendiendo,
hasta que por oriente, que ya dora,
relinchen los corceles de la aurora.

Do not be frightened, my love, for already the fire
is crackling against the wolves and the cold.
Throw it your heart of pure pearl
for mine burns so now with the logs;
and all through the night it will blaze
guarding your fear and defending your beauty,
until in the East, where gold drives the darkness away,
the chargers of dawn begin to neigh.

from *Poesía 1915-1956*, 1957
P.H.

Luis Palés Matos
DANZARINA AFRICANA

Tu belleza es profunda y confortante
como el ron de Jamaica, tu belleza
tiene la irrevelada fortaleza
del basalto, la brea y el diamante.

Tu danza es como un tósigo abrasante
de los filtros de la naturaleza,
y el deseo te enciende en la cabeza
su pirotecnia roja y detonante.

¡Oh negra densa y bárbara! Tu seno
esconde el salomónico veneno.
Y desatas terribles espirales,

cuando alrededor del macho resistente
te revuelves, porosa y absorbente,
como la arena de tus arenales.

Luis Palés Matos
AFRICAN DANCER

Your beauty is deep and comforting
like Jamaican rum, your beauty
has the unseen solidity
of basalt, tar and diamonds.

Your dance is like a burning poison
made of Nature's own love potions,
and desire ignites in your head
its red and fiery detonations.

Oh firm and barbarous black woman! Your breast
conceals a solomonic venom.
And you set loose terrible spirals,

when around the resistent male,
you circle, porous and absorbent
like the sand in your quicksand beds.

from *Poesía; 1915-1956*, 1957
P.H.

Nicanor Parra   *born in Chillán, Chile,*
                                 September 5, 1914

One of the best-known Chilean poets of the 20th century, Parra also
has had a career in engineering and as a mathematics and physics
professor. His iconoclastic, often humorous and satiric, narrative-like
style characterize the poems of *Poemas y antipoemas* (1954), his best
known book. An impetuous youth, he showed an early interest in
both literature and mathematics. It is said that when the famous
Gabriela Mistral came to Chilan to read her poems, Parra jumped
onto the stage to read *her* a poem he had written for her. Parra still
considers Chile his home, where he continues to write poetry, and to
work for the international ecology movement.

Nicanor Parra

ES OLVIDO

Juro que no recuerdo ni su nombre
mas moriré llamándola María,
no por simple capricho de poeta:
por su aspecto de plaza de provincia,
¡Tiempos aquellos! Yo un espantapájaros,
ella una joven pálida y sombría.
Al volver una tarde del Liceo
supe de la su muerte inmerecida,
nueva que me causó tal desengaño
que derramé una lágrima al oírla.
Una lágrima. Si. . . ¡Quién lo creyera!
Y eso que soy persona de energía.
Si he de conceder crédito a lo dicho
por la gente que trajo la noticia
debo creer sin vacilar un punto
que murió con mi nombre en las pupilas,
hecho que me sorprende porque nunca
fue para mí otra cosa que una amiga.
Nunca tuve con ella más que simples
relaciones de estricta cortesía:
nada más que palabras y palabras
y una que otra mención de golondrinas.
La conocí en mi pueblo (de mi pueblo
sólo queda un puñado de ceniza),
pero jamás vi en ella otro destino
que el de una joven triste y pensativa.
Tanto fue así que hasta llegué a tratarla
con el celeste nombre de María,
circunstancia que prueba claramente
la exactitud central de mi doctrina.
Puede ser que una vez la haya besado
¡Quién es el que no besa a sus amigas!
Pero tened presente que lo hice
sin darme cuenta bien de lo que hacía.
No negaré, eso sí, que me gustaba
su inmaterial y vaga compañía,

Nicanor Parra
FORGETFULNESS

I swear I don't even remember her name
but I'll die calling her Maria,
not for the simple caprice of a poet:
for the way she looked like a small town square,
those good times! I, a scarecrow,
she a young girl pale and somber.
Returning one afternoon from the lyceum
I found out about that undeserved death of hers,
news that caused me such disappointment
I shed a tear when I heard about it.
A tear. Yes ... who would believe it!
me being a person of such vigor.
If I have to give credit to what was said
by the people who brought the news
I ought to believe without any question
that she died with my name in her eyes,
a fact that surprised me because she was never
anything to me but a friend.
With her it was never more than the simple
relationship of strict courtesy;
nothing more than words and words
and here and there some mention of swallows.
I met her in my hometown (of my town
only a handful of ashes remains),
but I never saw in her any other destiny
than that of a sad and pensive young girl.
So much so that I even began to call her
by the celestial name of Maria,
a circumstance that clearly proves
the exact accuracy of my doctrine.
It's possible that I've kissed her once,
who doesn't kiss his friends!
But bear in mind I did it
without realizing what I was doing.
I won't deny, that's for sure, that I liked
her immaterial and vague company,

que era como el espíritu sereno
que a las flores domésticas anima.
Yo no puedo ocultar de ningún modo
la importancia que tuvo su sonrisa
ni denegar el favorable influjo
que hasta en las mismas piedras ejercía.
Agreguemos, aún, que de la noche
fueron sus ojos fuentes fidedignas.
Mas, a pesar de todo, es necesario
que comprendan que yo no la quería,
sino con ese vago sentimiento
con que a un pariente enfermo se designa.
Sin embargo sucede. Sin embargo,
lo que a esta fecha aún me maravilla,
ese inaudito y singular ejemplo
de morir con mi nombre en las pupilas
ella, múltiple rosa inmaculada,
ella, que era una lámpara legítima.
Tiene razón, mucha razón la gente
que se pasa quejando noche y día
de que el mundo traidor en que vivimos
vale menos que rueda detenida.
Mucho más honorable es una tumba,
vale más una hoja enmohecida.
Nada es verdad. Aquí nada perdura:
ni el color del cristal con que se mira.
Hoy es un día azul de primavera;
creo que moriré de poesía.
De esa famosa joven melancólica
no recuerdo ni el nombre que tenía.
Sólo sé que pasó por este mundo
como una paloma fugitiva.
La olvidé sin quererlo. Lentamente
como todas las cosas de la vida.

which was like the serene spirit
that makes household flowers come alive.
I can't hide in any way
the importance of her smile
nor deny the favorable influence
that she exercised even on the stones themselves.
Let's add, also, that her eyes
were reliable fountains in the night.
But, in spite of everything, you must
understand I didn't love her
except with that vague feeling
you keep for a sick relative.
Nevertheless, it happens. Nevertheless
what still amazes me today,
that unheard of and singular example
of dying with my name in her eyes
she, multiple immaculate rose,
she, who was a legitimate light.
The people are right, very right
who always complain night and day
that the treacherous world we live in
is worth less than a stopped wheel.
Much more honorable is a tomb,
a moldy leaf is worth more.
Nothing is true. Here nothing lasts:
not even the color of glass with which we see ourselves.
Today is a blue day of Spring;
I believe I'll die of poetry.
I don't even remember the name
of that famous melancholic young girl.
I only know she passed through this world
like a fugitive dove.
I forgot her without wanting to. Slowly
as all things in life.

from *Poemas y antipoemas*, 1954
C. J.

Octavio Paz   *born in Mexico City, Mexico,*
                               March 31, 1914

Once a friend of André Breton, the influence of surrealism is still
evident in his poetry, along with strong echoes from native Mexican
mythology. His poems frequently combine a primordial magical
atmosphere with intellectual contemplation. Known for his poetry,
essays and criticism, he was born in Mexico City during the Mexican
Revolution, the son of a lawyer who had defended Emiliano Zapata.
Educated at the National Autonomous University of Mexico, he
published *Luna silvestre*, his first poems at the age of 19. He spent a
year in Spain working in relief efforts for civil war refugees and
participating in an antifascist conference. During the Second World
War, he taught in the United States, as he has on many occasions
since then. He served Mexico as a diplomat in France, Japan, and
India; but resigned in protest from the diplomatic corps after
government troops killed Mexican students who were protesting their
government's restrictions of personal freedoms during the Olympic
Games in Mexico City in 1968.

Octavio Paz
MÁS ALLÁ DEL AMOR

Todo nos amenaza:
el tiempo, que en vivientes fragmentos divide
al que fui
          del que seré,
como el machete a la culebra;
la conciencia, la transparencia traspasada,
la mirada ciega de mirarse mirar;
la palabras, guantes grises, polvo mental sobre la yerba,
                              el agua, la piel;
nuestros nombres, que entre tú y yo se levantan,
murallas de vacío que ninguna trompeta derrumba.

Ni el sueño y su pueblo de imágenes rotas,
ni el delirio y su espuma profética,
ni el amor con sus dientes y uñas nos bastan.
Más allá de nosotros,
en las fronteras del ser y el estar,
una vida más vida nos reclama.

Afuera la noche respira, se extiende,
llena de grandes hojas calientes,
de espejos que combaten:
frutos, garras, ojos, follajes,
espaldas que relucen,
cuerpos que se abren paso entre otros cuerpos.

Tiéndete aquí a la orilla de tanta espuma,
de tanta vida que se ignora y entrega:
tú también perteneces a la noche.
Extiéndete, blancura que respira,
late, oh estrella repartida,
copa,
pan que inclinas la balanza del lado de la aurora,
pausa de sangre entre este tiempo y otro sin medida.

Octavio Paz
BEYOND LOVE

Everything menaces us:
time, that divides into living fragments
who I was,
                from who I will be,
like a machete does to a snake;
consciousness, transparency transfixed,
the blind look of watching yourself look;
words, gray gloves, mental dust on the grass, water, skin;
our names, that rise up between you and me,
walls of emptiness that no trumpet can fell.

Neither dreams peopled with broken images,
nor delirium and its prophetic foam,
nor love with its teeth and claws, suffices.
Beyond us,
on the frontiers of being and time,
a greater life than life beckons us.

Outside the night breathes, it expands,
full of great hot leaves,
of mirrors in combat:
fruit, talons, eyes, foliage,
backs that glisten,
bodies that push their way through other bodies.

Lie down here on the edge of so much foam,
of so much life that does not know and surrenders:
you too belong to the night.
Stretch out, whiteness that breathes,
throb, oh portioned star,
cup,
bread that tips the balance to the side of the dawn,
pause of blood between this time and another
                                    without measure.

from *El girasol*; *1943-1948*, 1948
P.H.

191

Francisco de Quevedo

born in Madrid, Spain, September, 1580

*died in Villanueva de los Infantes,
Province of Ciudad Real,
September 8, 1645*

Francisco de Quevedo was the great satirist of Spain's Baroque,
known for his ironic style, and for attacking virtually all Spanish
Golden Age institutions in poems and in a famous picaresque novel,
El Buscón (1608). Unlike most of his works, one of his finest poems
"Amor constante más allá de la muerte," finds in man's love
something real, meaningful and lasting. Of noble birth, Quevedo
lived most of his youth in the royal court. He was a superb
swordsman, and he became an expert in ancient and modern
languages, and in the sciences. Fascinated by government and
appalled by the corruption of Philip III's court, he plunged into
politics and wrote satiric poems and pamphlets. In 1608, he was
imprisoned when his patron, the Duke of Osuna, displeased the
king; for Quevedo, never reluctant to speak his mind, this was the
first of many imprisonments. A bachelor until 53, his only marriage
lasted a scant eight months. The winter of 1644 was a hard one, and
Quevedo, suffering from wounds and sicknesses contracted in prison,
died the following year.

Francisco de Quevedo
DEFINIENDO AL AMOR

Es yelo abrasador, es fuego helado,
es herida que duele y no se siente,
es un soñado bien, un mal presente,
es un breve descanso muy cansado.

Es un descuido que nos da cuidado,
un cobarde, con nombre de valiente,
un andar solitario entre la gente,
un amar solamente ser amado.

Es una libertad encarcelada,
que dura hasta el postrero parasismo;
enfermedad que crece si es curada.

Este es el niño Amor, éste es su abismo.
¡Mirad cuál amistad tendrá con nada
el que en todo es contrario de sí mismo!

Francisco de Quevedo
DEFINING LOVE

It's ice that burns, it is frozen fire,
it's a wound that hurts and is not felt,
it's something well dreamt, an evil present,
it's a brief retiring, that quickly tires.

It's a carelessness that makes us care,
a walk alone among a crowd,
a loving only of being loved,
a coward, with a brave man's name.

It's a liberty locked up in prison,
that lasts until the last convulsion;
an illness which spreads if it's cured.

This is young Cupid, this his abyss.
Just see what friends he'll make with nothing,
who's in all things against himself!

About 1620
from *Obras completas*, 1932
P.H.

Francisco de Quevedo
AMOR CONSTANTE MÁS ALLÁ DE LA MUERTE

Cerrar podrá mis ojos la postrera
sombra que me llevare el blanco día,
y podrá desatar esta alma mía
hora a su afán ansioso lisonjera;

mas no de esotra parte en la ribera
dejará la memoria, en donde ardía;
nadar sabe mi llama la agua fría,
y perder el respeto a la ley severa.

Alma a quien todo un dios prisión ha sido,
venas que humor a tanto fuego han dado,
medulas que han gloriosamente ardido;

su cuerpo dejarán, no su cuidado;
serán ceniza, mas tendrá sentido:
polvo serán, mas polvo enamorado.

Francisco de Quevedo
CONSTANT LOVE EVEN
BEYOND DEATH

My eyes may close in the last remaining
shadows that banish the whiteness of day
and this soul of mine may be freed
at a moment pleasing to its anxious longing;

but it shall not, of that other place on shore
forsake its memory, where it used to burn;
my flame can brave the icy current
and the most severe of laws ignore.

Soul to whom a whole god was prison,
veins which have poured fuel to so great a fire,
marrow which has so gloriously burned;

their body they will leave, not their feeling,
they shall be ash, yet it will have meaning;
dust they shall be, yet dust in love.

About 1620
from *Obras completas*, 1932
P.H.

197

Pedro Salinas   *born in Madrid, Spain,*
                                 November 27, 1892

                                 died in Boston, December 4, 1951

The theme of love is ever-present in Pedro Salinas' works, from
Presagios (1923) and *Seguro azar* (1929) to his most popular *La voz a
ti debida* (1933) and *Razón del amor* (1936), particularly the everyday
feelings and changes in a relationship, expressed in clear and brief
images, often characterized by irony and paradox. Born in Madrid,
Salinas studied law and literature during his years at the University,
and was a professor of literature. During the First World War he
taught at the Sorbonne. He returned to Spain in the 1920s, and then
accepted a position as Lecturer in Spanish Literature at Cambridge
University. During the Spanish civil war, he left Spain and went to
the United States, where he first taught at Wellesley College and then
spent many years at Johns Hopkins University.

Pedro Salinas
MIEDO

Miedo. De ti. Quererte
es el más alto riesgo.
Múltiples, tú y tu vida.
Te tengo, a la de hoy;
ya la conozco, entro
por laberintos, fáciles
gracias a ti, a tu mano.
Y míos ahora, sí.
Pero tú eres
tu propio más allá,
como la luz y el mundo:
días, noches, estíos,
inviernos sucediéndose.
Fatalmente, te mudas
sin dejar de ser tú,
en tu propia mudanza,
con la fidelidad
constante del cambiar.

Di, ¿podré yo vivir
en esos otros climas,
o futuros, o luces
que estás elaborando,
como su zumo el fruto,
para mañana tuyo?
¿O seré sólo algo
que nació para un día
tuyo (mi día eterno),
para una primavera
(en mí florida siempre),
sin poder vivir ya
cuando lleguen
sucesivas en ti,
inevitablemente,

Pedro Salinas
FEAR

Fear. Of you. Loving you
is the highest risk.
Multiple, you and your life.
I have you, today's you;
I know her now, I enter
through labyrinths, easy
thanks to you, to your hand.
And mine now, yes.
But you are
your own beyond
like light and the world:
days, nights, summers,
winters succeeding themselves.
Fatally, you change
without ceasing to be you,
in your own change,
with the constant fidelity
of change itself.

Tell me, will I be able to live
in those other climes,
or futures, or lights
that you are elaborating
like fruit does its juice,
for your tomorrow?
Or will I be only something
that was born for one day
of yours (my eternal day),
for one Spring
(in me forever in flower)
without being able to live any more
when there arrive
successive in you,
inevitably,

las fuerzas y los vientos
nuevos, las otras lumbres,
que esperan ya el momento
de ser, en ti, tu vida?

new forces and new winds,
other lights,
that already await the moment
of being, in you, your life?

from *La voz a ti debida*, 1933
P.H.

Pedro Salinas
¿SERÁS, AMOR . . .

¿Serás, amor,
un largo adiós que no se acaba?
Vivir, desde el principio, es separarse.
En el primer encuentro
con la luz, con los labios,
el corazón percibe la congoja
de tener que estar ciego y solo un día.
Amor es el retraso milagroso
de su término mismo:
es prolongar el hecho mágico
de que uno y uno sean dos, en contra
de la primera condena de la vida.
Con los besos,
con la pena y el pecho se conquistan,
en afanosas lides, entre gozos
parecidos a juegos,
días, tierras, espacios fabulosos,
a la gran disyunción que está esperando,
hermana de la muerte o muerte misma.
Cada beso perfecto aparta el tiempo,
la echa hacia atrás, ensancha el mundo breve
donde puede besarse todavía.
Ni en el llegar, ni en el hallazgo
tiene el amor su cima:
es en la resistencia a separarse
en donde se le siente,
desnudo, altísimo, temblando.
Y la separación no es el momento
cuando brazos, o voces,
se despiden con señas materiales:
es de antes, de después.
Si se estrechan las manos, si se abraza,
nunca es para apartarse,

Pedro Salinas
I WONDER, LOVE . . .

I wonder, love, are you
a long farewell that never ends?
From the first, living is separating.
In the first encounter
with light, with lips,
the heart perceives the anguish
of having to be blind and alone some day.
Love is the miraculous delay
of its own termination:
it is prolonging the magical fact
that one and one are two, in the face of
the original sentence of life.
With kisses,
with pain and the heart, we conquer
in eager disputes, among delights
that seem like games,
days, lands, fabulous spaces,
the great disjunction that is waiting,
the sister of death or death itself.
Each perfect kiss sets aside time,
casts it behind, extends the brief world
where one can still be kissed.
Not in arrival, nor in discovery
does love reach its summit:
it is in the resistance to parting
where you can feel it,
naked, exalted, trembling.
And separation is not the moment
when arms, or voices,
bid farewell with material signs;
it is from before, from after.
If hands are clasped, if we embrace,
it is never so we can leave,

es porque el alma ciegamente siente
que la forma posible de estar juntos
es una despedida larga, clara.
Y que lo más seguro es el adiós.

it is because the soul blindly feels
that the possible form of being together
is a long, clear farewell.
And that the most certain thing is goodbye.

from *Razón de amor,* 1936
P.H.

Pedro Salinas
LA DISTRAIDA

No estás ya aquí. Lo que veo
de ti, cuerpo, es sombra, engaño.
El alma tuya se fué
donde tú te irás mañana.
Aun esta tarde me ofrece
falsos rehenes, sonrisas
vagas, ademanes lentos,
un amor ya distraído.
Pero tu intención de ir
te llevó donde querías,
lejos de aquí, donde estás
diciéndome:
"Aquí estoy contigo, mira."
Y me señalas la ausencia.

Pedro Salinas
DISTRACTED

You are no longer here. What I see
of you, body, is shadow, deceit.
Your soul has gone away
where you will go tomorrow.
Yet even this afternoon offers me
false hostages, vague smiles,
slow gestures,
an already distracted love.
But your intention of going
took you where you wanted,
far from here, where you are
saying to me:
"Here I am with you, look."
And you show me your absence.

from *Seguro azar*, 1929
P.H.

Alfonsina Storni

born in May, 1892

died in Mar del Plata, Argentina,
October 25, 1938

Alfonsina Storni was born at sea, as her family sailed for Switzerland, her father's native country. Soon back in Argentina, she worked for the family cafe, in a hat factory, as an actress, and as a rural school teacher. Throughout many difficulties as a young woman, including the birth of her son, Alejandro (she never married), she remained determined to be a poet. The first of her poetry books, *La Inquietud del rosal* (1916) was widely acclaimed in literary circles. The most prevalent theme in Alfonsina Storni's poems is passionate relationships between men and women, characterized by intensely lyric style that sarcastically attacks established attitudes toward women. Dying of cancer, Storni took a train to Mar del Plata after mailing "Voy a dormir" to the Buenos Aires paper *La Nación*. She walked into the sea for the last time; her body was found at La Perla beach the next day.

Alfonsina Storni
TU ME QUIERES BLANCA

Tú me quieres alba,
me quieres de espumas,
me quieres de nácar.
Que sea azucena
sobre todas, casta.
De perfume tenue.
Corola cerrada.

Ni un rayo de luna
filtrado me haya.
Ni una margarita
se diga mi hermana.
Tú me quieres nívea,
tú me quieres blanca,
tú me quieres alba.

Tú que hubiste todas
las copas a mano,
de frutos y mieles
los labios morados.
Tú que en el banquete
cubierto de pámpanos
dejaste las carnes
festejando a Baco.
Tú que en los jardines
negros del engaño
vestido de rojo
corriste al estrago.
Tú que el esqueleto
conservas intacto
no sé todavía
por cuáles milagros,
me pretendes blanca
(Dios te lo perdone),
me pretendes casta
(Dios te lo perdone),
¡me pretendes alba!

Alfonsina Storni
YOU WANT ME WHITE

You want me white,
you want me foam,
you want me pearl.
That I would be white lily,
above all the others, chaste.
Of tenuous perfume.
Closed corolla.

That not even a ray of filtered
moonlight have me.
Nor a daisy
call itself my sister.
You want me snowy,
you want me white,
you want me dawn.

You who had all
the cups in hand,
Your lips purple
with fruits and honey.
You who at the banquet
covered with ferns
relinquished your flesh
celebrating Bacchus.
You who in black
gardens of deceit
dressed in red
ran yourself to ruin.
You whose skeleton
is still intact
by what miracles
I'll never know,
you want me to be white
(God forgive you),
you want me to be chaste
(God forgive you),
you want me to be dawn!

Huye hacia los bosques;
vete a la montaña;
límpiate la boca;
vive en las cabañas;
toca con las manos
la tierra mojada;
alimenta el cuerpo
con raíz amarga;
bebe de las rocas;
duerme sobre escarcha;
renueva tejidos
con salitre y agua;

Habla con los pájaros
y lévate al alba.
Y cuando las carnes
te sean tornadas,
y cuando hayas puesto
en ellas el alma
que por las alcobas
se quedó enredada,
entonces, buen hombre,
preténdeme blanca,
preténdeme nívea,
preténdeme casta.

Go to the woods;
go to the mountains;
wash out your mouth;
live in a hut;
touch the damp earth
with your hands;
nourish your body
with bitter roots;
drink from stones;
sleep on frost;
restore your body
with saltpeter and water;

Speak with birds
and get up at dawn.
And when your flesh
is restored to you,
and when you've put the soul
back into the flesh
which was entrapped
in bedrooms,
then, good man,
pretend I'm white,
pretend I'm snowy,
pretend I'm chaste.

from *El dulce daño*, 1918
C.J.

Alfonsina Storni
HOMBRE PEQUEÑITO

Hombre pequeñito, hombre pequeñito,
suelta a tu canario que quiere volar . . .
Yo soy el canario, hombre pequeñito,
déjame saltar.

Estuve en tu jaula, hombre pequeñito,
hombre pequeñito que jaula me das.
Digo pequeñito porque no me entiendes,
ni me entenderás.

Tampoco te entiendo, pero mientras tanto
ábreme la jaula que quiero escapar;
hombre pequeñito, te amé media hora,
no me pidas más.

Alfonsina Storni
LITTLE MAN

Little man, oh little man
Don't hold your canary so tight, it wants to fly . . .
I am the canary, oh little man,
Let me jump and play.

You had me in your cage, little man,
Little man, provider of my cage,
I say little man because you don't know me,
Nor will you ever manage.

Neither do I know you, but meanwhile
Throw open the cage, for I want to fly free;
little man, I loved you half an hour,
Don't ask any more of me.

from *Irremediablemente*, 1919
P.H.

Alfonsina Storni
EPITAFIO PARA MI TUMBA

Aquí descanso yo: dice Alfonsina
el epitafio claro, al que se inclina.

Aquí descanso yo, y en este pozo,
pues que no siento, me solazo y gozo.

Los turbios ojos muertos ya no giran,
los labios, desgranados, no suspiran.

Duermo mi sueño eterno a pierna suelta,
me llaman y no quiero darme vuelta.

Tengo la tierra encima y no la siento,
llega el invierno y no me enfría el viento.

El verano mis sueños no madura,
la primavera el pulso no me apura.

El corazón no tiembla, salta o late,
fuera estoy de la línea de combate.

¿Qué dice el ave aquélla, caminante?
Tradúceme su canto pertubante:

"Nace la luna nueva, el mar perfuma,
los cuerpos bellos báñanse de espuma.

Va junto al mar un hombre que en la boca
lleva una abeja libadora y loca:

bajo la blanca tela el torso quiere
el otro torso que palpita y muere.

Los marineros sueñan en las proas,
cantan muchachas desde las canoas.

Alfonsina Storni
EPITAPH FOR MY TOMB

Here I lie at rest: *Alfonsina* says
The well-carved epitaph, to passersby.

Here I lie at rest, and in this pit,
Since I have no feeling, I have solace and I enjoy it.

My turbid eyes in death no longer shine,
My lips, slightly parted, do not sigh.

I sleep my carefree eternal slumber,
They call but I don't want to answer.

There is dirt upon me but I cannot feel,
Winter comes and the winds no longer chill.

The summer does not ripen my dreams,
My pulse does not quicken in the Spring.

My heart does not flutter, skip or quake,
I am no more in the midst of the fray.

What does that bird say to the living?
Explain to me his perturbing song:

"The new moon is born, the sea perfumed,
Beautiful bodies are bathed in the foam.

A man walks by the sea and he carries,
In his mouth a bee, drunken and crazy.

Beneath the white clothes the torso desires
The other torso that throbs and dies.

Seafarers dream in the prows of their ships,
Young girls sing their songs from their skiffs.

Zarpan los buques y en sus claras cuevas
los hombres parten hacia tierras nuevas.

La mujer, que en el suelo está dormida,
y en su epitafio ríe de la vida,

como es mujer, grabó en su sepultura
una mentira aún: la de su hartura.''

The ships set sail and in their holds below,
Men leave for lands they do not know.

The woman who sleeps beneath earth's strife,
And in her epitaph laughs at life,

Since she is a woman on her tomb she inscribed
Still another lie: that she was ever satisfied."

from *Ocre*, 1925
P.H.

Alfonsina Storni
VOY A DORMIR

Dientes de flores, cofia de rocío,
manos de hierbas, tú, nodriza fina,
tenme prestas las sábanas terrosas
y el edredón de musgos escardados.

Voy a dormir, nodriza mía, acuéstame.
Ponme una lámpara a la cabecera;
una constelación; la que te guste;
todas son buenas; bájala un poquito,

Déjame sola: oyes romper los brotes . . .
te acuna un pie celeste desde arriba
y un pájaro te traza unos compases

para que olvides . . . Gracias. Ah, un encargo:
si él llama nuevamente por teléfono
le dices que no insista, que he salido . . .

Alfonsina Storni
I'M GOING TO SLEEP

Teeth of flowers, coif of dew,
hands of grasses, you, gentle nurse,
turn down the earthy sheets
and the eiderdown of weeded mosses.

I'm going to sleep, nurse, put me to bed.
Put a lamp at the headboard;
a constellation, whichever one you like;
they're all nice; turn it down a little.

Leave me alone: you can hear the tender shoots . . .
a celestial foot is rocking you from above
and a bird is tapping out some rhythms

so you can forget . . . Thank you . . . Oh yes, a message:
if he calls again on the phone
tell him not to keep trying, tell him I've gone out.

24th of October 1938
from *Obra poética completa,* 1964
P.H.

César Vallejo

born in Santiago de Chuco, Perú,
March 16, 1892

died in Paris, April 15, 1938

A love for humanity and compassion for all its suffering and misery is at the heart of César Vallejo's best poems. His *Poemas humanos* (1938), and *España, aparta de mí este cáliz* (1939), echo the pessimism of the earlier *Los heraldos negros* (1918), but with more personal and specific experiences, particularly the Spanish civil war. Youngest of 11 children, he was born into a mestizo family in Northern Peru. He studied medicine and worked on a sugar plantation in Trujillo before arriving in Lima in 1918. At 31, he left Peru for Paris, living in self-exile as a journalist and Spanish teacher. He married there and became active in the Communist Party. In 1930 his militant political activities led to his expulsion from France. He stayed in Madrid until the civil war broke out in 1936, and on returning to Paris spoke out against fascism and worked with relief efforts for Spanish refugees. Many of his greatest poems were published posthumously.

César Vallejo
CONSIDERANDO EN FRIO, IMPARCIALMENTE...

Considerando en frío, imparcialmente,
que el hombre es triste, tose y, sin embargo,
se complace en su pecho colorado;
que lo único que hace es componerse
de días;
que es lóbrego mamífero y se peina...

Considerando
que el hombre procede suavemente del trabajo
y repercute jefe, suena subordinado;
que el diagrama del tiempo
es constante diorama en sus medallas
y, a medio abrir, sus ojos estudiaron,
desde lejanos tiempos,
su forma famélica de masa...

Comprendiendo sin esfuerzo
que el hombre se queda, a veces, pensando,
como queriendo llorar,
y, sujeto a tenderse como objeto,
se hace buen carpintero, suda, mata
y luego canta, almuerza, se abotona...

Considerando también
que el hombre es en verdad un animal
y, no obstante, al voltear, me da con su tristeza
en la cabeza...

Examinando, en fin,
sus encontradas piezas, su retrete,
su desesperación, al terminar su día atroz, borrándolo...

Comprendiendo
que él sabe que le quiero,
que le odio con afecto y me es, en suma, indiferente...

César Vallejo
CONSIDERING COLDLY,
IMPARTIALLY . . .

Considering coldly, impartially,
that man is sad, he coughs and, nevertheless,
he's pleased in his crimson breast;
that all he ever does is put himself together
with days;
that he is a sullen mammal and he combs his hair . . .

Considering
that man behaves quietly at work
and echoes the boss, sounds subordinate;
that his diagram of time
is a continual diorama in his medals
and, through tired eyes, he has studied,
down through the ages,
his form in the famished masses of man . . .

Understanding without effort
that man is left, at times, thinking,
as if trying to weep,
and, subject to offering himself as an object,
he makes a good carpenter, he sweats, he kills
and then he sings, lunches, and buttons up . . .

Considering as well that man is in truth an animal
and, nevertheless, as he turns around, he hits me square
                    in the face with his sadness . . . .

Examining, finally,
his encountered fragments, his bathroom,
his desperation, when he finishes his atrocious day,
                    erasing it . . . .

Understanding
that he knows that I love him,
that I despise him with affection and he is to me, after all,
                    indifferent . . . .

Considerando sus documentos generales
y mirando con lentes aquel certificado
que prueba que nació muy pequeñito...

le hago una seña,
viene,
y le doy un abrazo, emocionado.
Qué más da! Emocionado... Emocionado...

Considering his general documents
and looking with eyeglasses at that certificate
that proves he was born very small . . . .

I motion to him,
he comes over,
and I give him an embrace, moved.
What the hell. Moved . . . deeply moved . . . .

from *Poemas humanos*, 1939
P.H.

César Vallejo

MASA

Al fin de la batalla,
y muerto el combatiente, vino hacia él un hombre
y le dijo: "No mueras; te amo tánto!"
Pero el cadáver ¡ay! siguió muriendo.

Se le acercaron dos y repitiéronle:
"No nos dejes! ¡Valor! ¡Vuelve a la vida!"
Pero el cadáver ¡ay! siguió muriendo.

Acudieron a él veinte, cien, mil, quinientos mil,
clamando: "Tánto amor, y no poder
                            nada contra la muerte!"
Pero el cadáver ¡ay! siguió muriendo.

Le rodearon millones de individuos,
con un ruego común: "Quédate, hermano!"
Pero el cadáver ¡ay! siguió muriendo.

Entonces, todos los hombres de la tierra
le rodearon; les vió el cadáver triste, emocionado;
incorporóse lentamente,
abrazó al primer hombre; echóse a andar . . .

César Vallejo
MASSES

At the end of the battle,
and the soldier dead, there came to him a man,
and he said, "Do not die; I love you so!"
But the dead body, ah! kept on dying.

Two approached him and repeated:
Do not leave us! Courage! Come back to life!
But the dead body, ah! kept on dying.

There came to him twenty, a hundred, a thousand,
                         five hundred thousand,
clamoring: "So much love, and no power at all
                         against death!"
But the dead body, ah! kept on dying.

Millions of individuals surrounded him,
with a common plea: "Stay with us, brother!"
But the dead body, ah! kept on dying.

Then, all the men of the earth
gathered around him; the sad dead man saw them,
                         very moved;
he rose up slowly,
embraced the first man; and began to walk . . .

from *España, aparta de mí este cáliz*, 1939
C.J. and P.H.

Xavier Villaurrutia   *born in Mexico City, Mexico,*
                          March 27, 1903

                          died in Mexico City, December 25, 1950

Xavier Villaurrutia was the founder of the first experimental theater
in Mexico City. He wrote plays, poetry, and lyrics to popular songs;
he also taught at the National University. He considered himself
mainly a poet, though his dramatic works are better known. His
poems show the influence of surrealism and his paradoxical style
achieves a profound feeling of the complications of life and love. A
notable satirist, he was acclaimed for his sharp wit. He never
married, living all his life with his mother and sisters in Colonia
Roma, and keeping an apartment in downtown Mexico City, where
he wrote and received guests. Known for his intellect, he was also
superstitious. He so feared being buried alive that he made friends
promise to see that he was dead before he was buried. And, in accord
with his wishes, after he died a vein was opened in his arm.

Xavier Villaurrutia
NOCTURNO DE LOS ANGELES

Se diría que las calles fluyen dulcemente en la noche.
Las luces no son tan vivas que logren desvelar el secreto,
el secreto que los hombres que van y vienen conocen,
porque todos están en el secreto
y nada se ganaría con partirlo en mil pedazos
si, por el contrario, es tan dulce guardarlo
y compartirlo sólo con la persona elegida.

Si cada uno dijera en un momento dado,
en sólo una palabra, lo que piensa,
las cinco letras del DESEO formarían una enorme
cicatriz luminosa,
una constelación más antigua, más viva aún
que las otras,
Y esa constelación sería como un ardiente sexo
en el profundo cuerpo de la noche,
o, mejor, como los Gemelos que por vez primera
en la vida
se miraran de frente, a los ojos, y se abrazaran
ya para siempre.

De pronto el río de la calle se puebla de sedientos seres.
Caminan, se detienen, prosiguen.
Cambian miradas, atreven sonrisas.
Forman imprevistas parejas . . .

Hay recodos y bancos de sombra,
orillas de indefinibles formas profundas
y súbitos huecos de luz que ciega
y puertas que ceden a la presión más leve.

El río de la calle queda desierto un instante.
Luego parece remontar de sí mismo
deseoso de volver a empezar.
Queda un momento paralizado, mudo anhelante
como el corazón entre dos espasmos.

Xavier Villaurrutia
LOS ANGELES NOCTURNE

It looks like the streets are flowing sweetly in the night.
The lights are not so bright as to unveil the secret,
the secret known to the men who come and go
because they are all in on the secret
and nothing would be gained by dividing it into
a thousand pieces
if, on the contrary, it is so sweet to keep it
and share it only with one chosen person.

If everyone said at one given moment,
in just one word, what they were thinking,
the six letters of DESIRE would form a great luminous scar,
a more ancient constellation, brighter than the others.
And that constellation would be like the
hungering genitals
on the deep body of the night,
or, better yet, like the Gemini that for the first time
in their lives
would look at each other face to face, eye to eye,
and embrace forever.

Suddenly the river of the street fills with thirsty beings.
They walk, they stop, they go on.
They look at each other, they dare to smile.
Couples form by chance.

There are shadowy corners and benches,
sidewalks with undefinable deep shapes
and sudden hollows of blinding light
and doors that yield to the slightest touch.

The river of the street is deserted for an instant.
Then it seems to rise from itself
desirous to begin again.
It is paralyzed for a moment, mute, eager
like a heart between two spasms.

Pero una nueva pulsación, un nuevo latido
arroja al río de la calle nuevos sedientos seres.
Se cruzan, se entrecruzan y suben.
Vuelan a ras de tierra.

Nadan de pie, tan milagrosamente
que nadie se atrevería a decir que no caminan.
Son los Angeles.
Han bajado a la tierra
por invisibles escalas.
Vienen del mar, que es el espejo del cielo,
en barcos de humo y sombra,
a fundirse y confundirse con los mortales,
a rendir sus frentes en los muslos de las mujeres,
a dejar que otras manos palpen sus cuerpos febrilmente,
y que otros cuerpos busquen los suyos hasta encontrarlos
como se encuentran al cerrarse los labios

                             de una misma boca,
a fatigar su boca tanto tiempo inactiva,
a poner en libertad sus lenguas de fuego,
a decir las canciones, los juramentos, las malas palabras
en que los hombres concentran el antiguo misterio
de la carne, la sangre, y el deseo.

Tienen nombres supuestos, divinamente sencillos.
Se llaman Dick o John, o Marvin o Louis.
En nada sino en la belleza se distinguen de los mortales.
Caminan, se detienen, prosiguen.
Cambian miradas, atreven sonrisas.
Forman imprevistas parejas.
Sonríen maliciosamente al subir en los ascensores

                             de los hoteles
donde aún se practica el vuelo lento y vertical.
En sus cuerpos desnudos hay huellas celestiales:
signos, estrellas y letras azules.
Se dejan caer en las camas, se hunden en las almohadas
que los hacen pensar todavía un momento en las nubes.

But a new pulsing, a new beating
casts new thirsty beings into the river of the street.
They crisscross past each other and rise.
They are flying along the ground.

They are swimming on foot, so miraculously
that no one would dare say they are not walking.
They are the Angels.
They have come down to earth
on invisible ladders.
They come from the sea, which is the mirror of the sky,
in ships of smoke and shadow,
to meld and blend in with the mortals,
to surrender their foreheads on women's thighs,
to let other hands touch their bodies feverishly,
and other bodies seek theirs until they find them
as lips in the same mouth meet when they close,
to tire out their long inactive mouths,
to set their fiery tongues free,
to say the songs, the oaths, the profanity
in which men concentrate the ancient mystery
of flesh, blood, and desire.

Their names are false, divinely simple.
They call themselves Dick or John, or Marvin or Louis.
They only differ from mortals in their beauty.
They walk, they stop, they go on.
They look at each other, they dare to smile.
Couples form by chance.
They smile maliciously getting in the elevators in hotels
where slow and vertical flight is still possible.
On their naked bodies there are traces of heaven:
marks, stars and blue letters.
They let themselves fall into bed, they sink into
                                        the pillows
that still remind them for a moment of the clouds.

Pero cierran los ojos para entregarse mejor a los goces
de su encarnación misteriosa,
y cuando duermen sueñan no con los ángeles sino
con los mortales.

Los Angeles, California

But they close their eyes to better yield to the joys
                         of their mysterious incarnation,
and when they sleep they will not dream of angels
                                    but of mortals.

from *Nocturnos*, 1933
P.H.

Xavier Villaurrutia
NUESTRO AMOR

Si nuestro amor no fuera,
al tiempo que un secreto,
un tormento, una duda,
una interrogación;

si no fuera una larga
espera interminable,
un vacío en el pecho
donde el corazón llama
como un puño cerrado
a una puerta impasible;

si nuestro amor no fuera
el sueño doloroso
en que vives sin mí,
dentro de mí, una vida
que me llena de espanto;

si no fuera un desvelo,
un grito iluminado
en la noche profunda;

si nuestro amor no fuera
como un hilo tendido
en que vamos los dos
sin red sobre el vacío;

si tus palabras fueran
sólo palabras para
nombrar con ellas cosas
tuyas, no más, y mías;

si no resucitaran,
si no evocaran trágicas
distancias y rencores
traspuestos y olvidados;

Xavier Villaurrutia
OUR LOVE

If our love were not,
at the same time a secret,
a torment, a doubt,
an interrogation;

if it were not a long
interminable wait,
an emptiness in the breast
where the heart beats
like a closed fist
on some impassive door;

if our love were not
the painful dream
in which you live without me,
inside me, a life
which fills me with fright;

if it were not sleeplessness,
an illumined cry
in the deep night;

if our love were not
like a tightrope
on which the two of us go
without a net over the void;

if your words were
only words for
naming things
of yours, nothing more, and mine;

if they did not revive,
if they did not evoke tragic
distances and rancors
transposed and forgotten;

si tu mirada fuera
siempre la que un instante
—¡pero qué instante eterno!—
es tu más honda entrega;

si tus besos no fueran
sino para mis labios
trémulos y sumisos;
si tu lenta saliva
no fundiera en mi boca
su sabor infinito;

si juntos nuestros labios
desnudos como cuerpos,
y nuestros cuerpos juntos
como labios desnudos
no formaran un cuerpo
y una respiración,
¡no fuera amor el nuestro,
no fuera nuestro amor!

if your look were
always the one that for an instant
—but what an eternal instant!—
is your deepest surrender;

if your kisses were not
for any lips but mine
trembling and submissive;
if your lingering saliva
did not blend in my mouth
its infinite taste;

if together our lips
naked like bodies,
and our bodies together
like naked lips
did not form one body
and one breath,
ours would not be love,
our love would not be!

from *Canto a la primavera y otros poemas*, 1948
P.H.

243